Dale Carnegie's

14 Day Worry Cure

Dale Carnegie's
14 DAY
WORRY CURE

Containing

What Worry May Do to You

THE GREAT Nobel prize winner in medicine, Dr. Alexis Carrel, said, "Businessmen who do not know how to fight worry die young." And so do housewives and horse doctors and bricklayers.

A few years ago, I spent my vacation motoring through Texas and New Mexico with Dr. O. F. Gober—one of the medical executives of the Santa Fe railway. His exact title was chief physician of the Gulf, Colorado and Santa Fe Hospital Association. We got to talking about the effects of worry, and he said: "Seventy per cent of all patients who come to physicians could cure themselves if they only got rid of their fears and worries. Don't think for a moment that I mean that their ills are imaginary," he said. "Their ills are as real as a throbbing toothache and sometimes a hundred times more serious. I refer to such illnesses as nervous indigestion, some stomach ulcers, heart disturbances, insomnia, some headaches, and some types of paralysis."

Worry can make even the most stolid person ill. General Grant discovered that during the closing days of the Civil War. The story goes like this: Grant had been besieging Richmond for nine months. General Lee's troops, ragged and hungry, were beaten. Entire regiments were deserting at a time. Others were holding prayer meetings in their tents—shouting, weeping, and seeing visions. The end was close. Lee's men set fire to the cotton and tobacco warehouses in Richmond, burned the arsenal, and fled from the city at night while towering flames roared up into darkness. Grant was in hot pursuit, banging away at the Confederates from both sides and the rear, while Sheridan's cavalry was heading them off in front, tearing up railway lines and capturing supply trains.

Grant, half blind with a violent sick headache, fell behind his army and stopped at a farmhouse. "I spent the night," he records in his *Memoirs*, "in bathing my feet in hot water and mustard, and putting mustard plasters on my wrists and the back part of my neck, hoping to be cured by morning."

The next morning, he was cured instantaneously. And the thing that cured him was not a mustard plaster, but a horseman galloping down the road with a letter from Lee, saying he wanted to surrender.

"When the officer [bearing the message] reached me," Grant wrote, "I was still suffering with the sick headache, but the instant I saw the contents of the note, I was cured."

Obviously it was Grant's worries, tensions, and emotions that made him ill. He was cured instantly the moment his emotions took on the hue of confidence, achievement, and victory.

3

MERLE OBERON ON WORRY AND BEAUTY

When I interviewed Merle Oberon, she told me that she refused to worry because she knew that worry would destroy her chief asset on the motion-picture screen: her good looks.

"When I first tried to break into the movies," she told me, "I was worried and scared. I had just come from India, and I didn't know anyone in London, where I was trying to get a job. I saw a few producers, but none of them hired me; and the little money I had began to give out. For two weeks I lived on nothing but crackers and water. I was not only worried now. I was hungry. I said to myself, 'Maybe you're a fool. Maybe you will *never* break into the movies. After all, you have no experience, you've never acted at all—what have you to offer but a rather pretty face?'

"I went to the mirror. And when I looked in that mirror, I saw what worry was doing to my looks! I saw the lines it was forming. I saw the anxious expression. So I said to myself, 'You've got to stop this at once! You can't afford to worry. The only thing you have to offer at all is your looks, and worry will ruin them!'"

Few things can age and sour a woman and destroy her looks as quickly as worry. Worry curdles the expression. It makes us clench our jaws and lines our faces with wrinkles. It forms a permanent scowl. It may turn the hair gray, and, in some cases, even make it fall out. It can ruin the complexion—it can bring on all kinds of skin rashes, eruptions, and pimples.

Do you love life? Do you want to live long and enjoy good health? Here is how you can do it. I am quoting Dr. Alexis Carrel again: He said, *"Those who keep the peace of their inner selves in the midst of the tumult of the modern city are immune from nervous diseases."*

Rule 1: Remind yourself of the exorbitant price you can pay for worry in terms of your health. "Businessmen who do not know how to fight worry die young."

Live in "Day-tight Compartments"

IN THE SPRING of 1871, a young man picked up a book and read twenty-one words that had a profound effect on his future. A medical student at the Montreal General Hospital, he was worried about passing the final examination, worried about what to do, where to go, how to build up a practice, how to make a living.

The twenty-one words that this young medical student read in 1871 helped him to become the most famous physician of his generation. When he died, two huge volumes containing 1466 pages were required to tell the story of his life.

21 MAGIC WORDS

His name was Sir William Osler. Here are the twenty-one words that he read in the spring of 1871—twenty-one words from Thomas Carlyle that helped him lead a life free from worry: *Our main business is not to see what lies dimly at a distance, but to do what lies clearly at hand.*

Forty-two years later, on a soft spring night when the tulips were blooming on the campus, this man, Sir William Osler, addressed the students of Yale University. He told those Yale students that a man like himself who had been a professor in four universities and had written a popular book was supposed to have "brains of a special quality." He declared that that was untrue. He said that his intimate friends knew that his brains were "of the most mediocre character."

What, then, was the secret of his success? He stated that it was owing to what he called living in "day-tight compartments." What did he mean by that? A few months before he spoke at Yale, Sir William Osler had crossed the Atlantic on a great ocean liner where the captain, standing on the bridge, could press a button and—presto!—there was a clanging of machinery and various parts of the ship were immediately shut off from one another—shut off into watertight compartments. "Now each one of you," Dr. Osler said to those Yale students, "is a much more marvellous organization than the great liner, and bound on a longer voyage. What I urge is that you so learn to control the machinery as to live with 'day-tight compartments' as the most certain way to ensure safety on the voyage. Get on the bridge, and see that at least the great bulkheads are in working order. Touch a button and hear, at every level of your life, the iron doors shutting out the Past—the dead yesterdays. Touch another and shut off, with a metal curtain, the Future—the unborn tomorrows. Then you are safe—safe for to-day! . . . Shut off the past! Let the dead past bury its dead. . . . Shut out the yesterdays which have lighted fools the way to dusty death. . . . The load of tomorrow, added to that of yesterday, carried today, makes the strongest falter. Shut off the future as tightly as the past. . . . The future is today. . . . There is no tomorrow. The day of man's salvation is now. Waste of energy, mental distress, nervous worries dog the steps of a man who is anxious about the future. . . . Shut close, then, the great fore and aft bulkheads, and prepare to cultivate the habit of a life of 'day-tight compartments.'"

Sir William Osler urged the students at Yale to begin the day with Christ's prayer: "Give us this day our daily bread."

Remember that that prayer asks only for *today's* bread. It doesn't complain about the stale bread we had to eat yesterday; and it doesn't say: "Oh, God, it has been pretty dry out in the wheat belt lately and we may have another drought—and then how will I get bread to eat next fall—or suppose I lose my job—oh, God, how could I get bread then?"

No, this prayer teaches us to ask for *today's* bread only. Today's bread is the only kind of bread you can possibly eat.

Years ago, a penniless philosopher was wandering through a stony country where the people had a hard time making a living. One day a crowd gathered about him on a hill, and he gave what is probably the most-quoted speech ever delivered anywhere at any time. This speech contains twenty-six words that have gone ringing down across the centuries: "Take therefore no thought for the morrow; for the morrow shall take thought for the things of itself. Sufficient unto the day is the evil thereof."

Many men have rejected those words of Jesus: "Take no thought for the morrow." They have rejected those words as a counsel of perfection, as a bit of Oriental mysticism. "I *must* take thought for the morrow," they say. "I *must* take out insurance to protect my family. I *must* lay aside money for my old age. I *must* plan and prepare to get ahead."

Right! Of course you must. The truth is that those words of Jesus, translated over three hundred years ago, don't mean today what they meant during the reign of King James. Three hundred years ago the word *thought* frequently meant anxiety. Modern versions of the Bible quote Jesus more accurately as saying: "Have no anxiety for the tomorrow."

By all means take thought for the tomorrow, yes, careful thought and planning and preparation. But have no anxiety.

During the war, our military leaders *planned* for the morrow, but they could not afford to have any anxiety. "I have supplied the best men with the best equipment we have," said Admiral Ernest J. King, who directed the United States Navy, "and have given them what seems to be the wisest mission. That is all I can do."

"If a ship has been sunk," Admiral King went on, "I can't bring it up. If it is going to be sunk, I can't stop it. I can use my time much better working on tomorrow's problem than by fretting about yesterday's. Besides, if I let those things get me, I wouldn't last long."

You and I are standing this very second at the meeting place of two eternities: the vast past that has endured forever, and the future that is plunging on to the last syllable of recorded time. We can't possibly live in either of those eternities—no, not even for one split second. But, by trying to do so, we can wreck both our bodies and our minds. So let's be content to live the only time we can possibly live: from now until bedtime. "Anyone can carry his

6

burden, however hard, until nightfall," wrote Robert Louis Stevenson. "Anyone can do his work, however hard, for one day. Anyone can live sweetly, patiently, lovingly, purely, till the sun goes down. And this is all that life really means."

A HOUSEWIFE'S EXPERIENCE

Yes, that is all that life requires of us; but Mrs. E. K. Shields, 815 Court Street, Saginaw, Michigan, was driven to despair—even to the brink of suicide —before she learned to live just till bedtime. "In 1937, I lost my husband," Mrs. Shields said as she told me her story. "I was very depressed—and almost penniless. I wrote my former employer, Mr. Leon Roach, of the Roach-Fowler Company of Kansas City, and got my old job back. I had formerly made my living selling World Books to rural and town school boards. I had sold my car two years previously when my husband became ill; but I managed to scrape together enough money to put a down payment on a used car and started out to sell books again.

"I had thought that getting back on the road would help relieve my depression; but driving alone and eating alone was almost more than I could take. Some of the territory was not very productive, and I found it hard to make those car payments, small as they were.

"In the spring of 1938, I was working out of Versailles, Missouri. The schools were poor, the roads bad; I was so lonely and discouraged that at one time I even considered suicide. It seemed that success was impossible. I had nothing to live for. I dreaded getting up each morning and facing life. I was afraid of everything: afraid I could not meet the car payments; afraid I could not pay my room rent; afraid I would not have enough to eat. I was afraid my health was failing and I had no money for a doctor. All that kept me from suicide were the thoughts that my sister would be deeply grieved, and that I did not have enough money to pay my funeral expenses.

"Then one day I read an article that lifted me out of my despondence and gave me the courage to go on living. I shall never cease to be grateful for one inspiring sentence in that article. It said: 'Every day is a new life to a wise man.' I typed that sentence out and pasted it on the windshield of my car, where I saw it every minute I was driving. I found it wasn't so hard to live only one day at a time. I learned to forget the yesterdays and to not-think of the tomorrows. Each morning I said to myself, 'Today is a new life.'

"I have succeeded in overcoming my fear of loneliness, my fear of want. I am happy and fairly successful now and have a lot of enthusiasm and love for life. I know now that I shall never again be afraid, regardless of what life hands me. I know now that I don't have to fear the future. I know now that I can live one day at a time—and that 'Every day is a new life to a wise man.'"

John Ruskin had on his desk a simple piece of stone on which was carved one word: TODAY. And while I haven't a piece of stone on my desk, I do have a poem pasted on my mirror where I can see it when I shave every morning— a poem that Sir William Osler always kept on his desk—a poem written by the famous Indian dramatist, Kalidasa:

SALUTATION TO THE DAWN

Look to this day!
For it is life, the very life of life.
In its brief course
Lie all the verities and realities of your existence:
    The bliss of growth
    The glory of action
    The splendor of achievement,
For yesterday is but a dream
And tomorrow is only a vision,
But today well lived makes every yesterday a dream of happiness
And every tomorrow a vision of hope.
Look well, therefore, to this day!
Such is the salutation to the dawn.

Rule 2: Shut the iron doors on the past and the future. Live in Day-tight Compartments.

Why not ask yourself these questions, and write down the answers?
1. Do I tend to put off living in the present in order to worry about the future, or to yearn for some "magical rose garden over the horizon"?
2. Do I sometimes embitter the present by regretting things that happened in the past—that are over and done with?
3. Do I get up in the morning determined to "Seize the day"—to get the utmost out of these twenty-four hours?
4. Can I get more out of life by "living in day-tight compartments"?
5. When shall I start to do this? Next week? . . . Tomorrow? . . . *Today?*

A Magic Formula for Solving Worry Situations

WOULD YOU like a quick, sure-fire recipe for handling worry situations—a technique you can start using right away, before you go any further in reading this book?

Then let me tell you about the method worked out by Willis H. Carrier, the

8

brilliant engineer who launched the air-conditioning industry, and who is now head of the world-famous Carrier Corporation, in Syracuse, New York. It is one of the best techniques I ever heard of for solving worry problems, and I got it from Mr. Carrier personally when we were having lunch together one day at the Engineers' Club in New York.

"When I was a young man," Mr. Carrier said, "I worked for the Buffalo Forge Company in Buffalo, New York. I was handed the assignment of installing a gas-cleaning device in a plant of the Pittsburgh Plate Glass Company at Crystal City, Missouri—a plant costing millions of dollars. The purpose of this installation was to remove the impurities from the gas so it could be burned without injuring the engines. This method of cleaning gas was new. It had been tried only once before—and under different conditions. In my work at Crystal City, Missouri, unforeseen difficulties arose. It worked after a fashion—but not well enough to meet the guarantee we had made.

"I was stunned by my failure. It was almost as if someone had struck me a blow on the head. My stomach, my insides, began to twist and turn. For a while I was so worried I couldn't sleep.

"Finally, common sense reminded me that worry wasn't getting me anywhere; so I figured out a way to handle my problem without worrying. It worked superbly. I have been using this same anti-worry technique for more than thirty years. It is simple. Anyone can use it. It consists of three steps:

"Step I. *I analyzed the situation fearlessly and honestly and figured out what was the worst that could possibly happen as a result of this failure.* No one was going to jail me or shoot me. That was certain. True, there was a chance that I would lose my position; and there was also a chance that my employers would have to remove the machinery and lose the twenty thousand dollars we had invested.

"Step II. *After figuring out what was the worst that could possibly happen, I reconciled myself to accepting it, if necessary.* I said to myself: This failure will be a blow to my record, and it might possibly mean the loss of my job; but if it does, I can always get another position. Conditions could be much worse; and as far as my employers are concerned—well, they realize that we are experimenting with a new method of cleaning gas, and if this experience costs them twenty thousand dollars, they can stand it. They can charge it up to research, for it is an experiment.

"After discovering the worst that could possibly happen and reconciling myself to accepting it, if necessary, an extremely important thing happened: I immediately relaxed and felt a sense of peace that I hadn't experienced in days.

"Step III. *From that time on, I calmly devoted my time and energy to trying to improve upon the worst which I had already accepted mentally.*

"I now tried to figure out ways and means by which I might reduce the loss of twenty thousand dollars that we faced. I made several tests and finally figured out that if we spent another five thousand for additional equipment, our problem would be solved. We did this, and instead of the firm losing twenty thousand, we made fifteen thousand.

"I probably would never have been able to do this if I had kept on worrying, because one of the worst features about worrying is that it destroys our ability to concentrate. When we worry, our minds jump here and there and everywhere, and we lose all power of decision. However, when we force ourselves to face the worst and accept it mentally, we then eliminate all these vague imaginings and put ourselves in a position in which we are able to concentrate on our problem.

"This incident that I have related occurred many years ago. It worked so superbly that I have been using it ever since; and, as a result, my life has been almost completely free from worry."

Now, why is Willis H. Carrier's magic formula so valuable and so practical, psychologically speaking? Because it yanks us down out of the great gray clouds in which we fumble around when we are blinded by worry. It plants our feet good and solid on the earth. We know where we stand. And if we haven't solid ground under us, how in creation can we ever hope to think anything through?

So, **Rule 3** is: If you have a worry problem, apply the magic formula of Willis H. Carrier by doing these three things—

1. **Ask yourself, "What is the worst that can possibly happen?"**
2. **Prepare to accept it if you have to.**
3. **Then calmly proceed to improve on the worst.**

What Causes Half the Worry in the World

THE LATE Herbert E. Hawkes, Dean of Columbia College, Columbia University, told me that *"confusion is the chief cause of worry."* He put it this way—he said: "Half the worry in the world is caused by people trying to make decisions before they have sufficient knowledge on which to base a decision. For example," he said, "if I have a problem which has to be faced at three o'clock next Tuesday, I refuse to even try to make a decision about it until next Tuesday arrives. In the meantime, I concentrate on getting all the facts that bear on the problem. I don't worry," he said. "I don't agonize over my problem. I don't lose any sleep. I simply concentrate on getting the facts. And by the time Tuesday rolls around, if I've got all the facts, the problem usually solves itself!"

I asked Dean Hawkes if this meant he had licked worry entirely. "Yes," he said, "I think I can honestly say that my life is now almost totally devoid of worry. I have found," he went on, "that if a man will devote his time to securing facts in an impartial, objective way, his worries will usually evaporate in the light of knowledge."

However, getting all the facts in the world won't do us any good until we analyze them and interpret them.

I have found from costly experience that it is much easier to analyze the facts after writing them down. In fact, merely writing the facts on a piece of paper and stating our problem clearly goes a long way toward helping us reach a sensible decision. As Charles Kettering puts it: "A problem well stated is a problem half solved."

Let me show you all this as it works out in practice. Since the Chinese say one picture is worth ten thousand words, suppose I show you a picture of how one man put exactly what we are talking about into concrete action.

Let's take the case of Frank Bettger, one of the top insurance men in America.

"Years ago," says Frank Bettger, "when I first started to sell insurance, I was filled with a boundless enthusiasm and love for my work. Then something happened. I became so discouraged that I despised my work and thought of giving it up. I think I would have quit—if I hadn't got the idea, one Saturday morning, of sitting down and trying to get at the root of my worries.

"1. I asked myself first, *'Just what is the problem?'* The problem was: *that I was not getting high enough returns for the staggering amount of calls I was making.* I seemed to do pretty well at selling a prospect, until the moment came for closing a sale. Then the customer would say, 'Well, I'll think it over, Mr. Bettger. Come and see me again.' It was the time I wasted on these follow-up calls that was causing my depression.

"2. I asked myself, *'What are the possible solutions?'* But to get the answer to that one, *I had to study the facts.* I got out my record book for the last twelve months and studied the figures.

"*I made an astounding discovery!* Right there in black and white, I discovered that seventy per cent of my sales had been closed on the very first interview! Twenty-three per cent of my sales had been closed on the second interview! And only *seven per cent of my sales* had been closed on those third, fourth, fifth, etc., interviews, which were running me ragged and taking up time. In other words, I was wasting fully one half of my working day

11

on a part of my business which was responsible for only seven per cent of my sales!

"3. *'What is the answer?'* The answer was obvious. I immediately cut out all visits beyond the second interview, and spent the extra time building up new prospects. The results were unbelievable. In a very short time, I had raised the cash value of every visit I made from $2.80 to $4.27 a call!"

As I said, Frank Bettger is now one of the best-known life-insurance salesmen in the country. He is with Fidelity Mutual of Philadelphia, and writes a million dollars' worth of policies a year. But he was on the point of giving up. He was on the point of admitting failure—until *analyzing* the problem gave him a boost on the road to success.

Here is another example, told to me by Leon Shimkin, a partner and general manager of one of the foremost publishing houses in these United States: Simon and Schuster, Rockefeller Center, New York 20, New York.

Here is Leon Shimkin's experience in his own words:

"For fifteen years I spent almost half of every business day holding conferences, discussing problems. Should we do this or that—do nothing at all? We would get tense; twist in our chairs; walk the floor; argue and go around in circles. When night came, I would be utterly exhausted. I fully expected to go on doing this sort of thing for the rest of my life. I had been doing it for fifteen years, and it never occurred to me that there was a better way of doing it. If anyone had told me that I could eliminate three fourths of all the time I spent in those worried conferences, and three fourths of my nervous strain—I would have thought he was a wild-eyed, slap-happy, armchair optimist. Yet I devised a plan that did just that. I have been using this plan for eight years. It has performed wonders for my efficiency, my health, and my happiness.

"It sounds like magic—but like all magic tricks, it is extremely simple when you see how it is done.

"Here is the secret: First, I immediately stopped the procedure I had been using in my conferences for fifteen years—a procedure that began with my troubled associates reciting all the details of what had gone wrong, and ending up by asking: 'What shall we do?' Second, I made a new rule—a rule that everyone who wishes to present a problem to me must first prepare and submit a memorandum answering these four questions:

"Question 1: *What is the problem?*

("In the old days we used to spend an hour or two in a worried conference without anyone's knowing specifically and concretely what the real problem was. We used to work ourselves into a lather discussing our troubles without ever troubling to write out specifically what our problem was.)

"Question 2: *What is the cause of the problem?*

("As I look back over my career, I am appalled at the wasted hours I have spent in worried conferences without ever trying to find out clearly the conditions which lay at the root of the problem.)

"Question 3: *What are all possible solutions of the problem?*

("In the old days, one man in the conference would suggest one solution. Someone else would argue with him. Tempers would flare. We would often get clear off the subject, and at the end of the conference no one would have written down all the various things we could do to attack the problem.)"

Neither you nor I nor Einstein nor the Supreme Court of the United States is brilliant enough to reach an intelligent decision on any problem without first getting the facts.

So here is question No. 1—*What am I worrying about?* (Please pencil the answer to that question in the space below.)

Question No. 2—*What can I do about It?* (Please write your answer to that question in the space below.)

Question No. 3—*Here is what I am going to do about it.*

How to Break the Worry Habit Before It Breaks You

I SHALL NEVER forget the night, a few years ago, when Marion J. Douglas was a student in one of my classes. He told us how tragedy had struck at his home, not once, but twice. The first time he had lost his five-year-old daughter, a child he adored. He and his wife thought they couldn't endure that first loss; but, as he said, "Ten months later God gave us another little girl—and she died in five days."

This double bereavement was almost too much to bear. "I couldn't take it," this father told us. "I couldn't sleep, I couldn't eat, I couldn't rest or relax. My nerves were utterly shaken and my confidence gone." At last he went to doctors; one recommended sleeping pills and another recommended a trip. He tried both, but neither remedy helped. He said, "My body felt as if it were encased in a vise, and the jaws of the vise were being drawn tighter and tighter." The tension of grief—if you have ever been paralyzed by sorrow, you know what he meant.

"But thank God, I had one child left—a four-year-old son. He gave me the solution to my problem. One afternoon as I sat around feeling sorry for myself, he asked: 'Daddy, will you build a boat for me?' I was in no mood to build a boat; in fact, I was in no mood to do anything. But my son is a persistent little fellow! I had to give in.

"Building that toy boat took about three hours. By the time it was finished, I realized that those three hours spent building that boat were the first hours of mental relaxation and peace that I had had in months!

"That discovery jarred me out of my lethargy and caused me to do a bit of thinking—the first real thinking I had done in months. I realized that it is difficult to worry while you are busy doing something that requires planning and thinking. In my case, building the boat had knocked worry out of the ring. So I resolved to keep busy.

"The following night, I went from room to room in the house, compiling a list of jobs that ought to be done. Scores of items needed to be repaired: bookcases, stair steps, storm windows, window shades, knobs, locks, leaky faucets. Astonishing as it seems, in the course of two weeks I had made a list of 242 items that needed attention.

"During the last two years I have completed most of them. Besides, I have filled my life with stimulating activities. Two nights per week I attend adult-education classes in New York. I have gone in for civic activities in my home town and I am now chairman of the school board. I attend scores of meetings. I help collect money for the Red Cross and other activities. I am so busy now that I have no time for worry."

Why does such a simple thing as keeping busy help to drive out anxiety? Because of a law—one of the most fundamental laws ever revealed by psychology. And that law is: that it is utterly impossible for any human mind, no matter how brilliant, to think of more than *one thing* at any given time. You don't quite believe it? Very well, then, let's try an experiment.

Suppose you lean back right now, close your eyes, and try, at the same instant, to think of the Statue of Liberty and of what you plan to do tomorrow morning. (Go ahead, try it.)

You found out, didn't you, that you could focus on either thought *in turn*, but never on both simultaneously? Well, the same thing is true in the field of emotions. We cannot be pepped up and enthusiastic about doing something exciting and feel dragged down by worry at the very same time. One kind of emotion drives out the other. And it was that simple discovery that enabled Army psychiatrists to perform such miracles during the war.

When men came out of battle so shaken by the experience that they were called "psychoneurotic," Army doctors prescribed "Keep 'em busy" as a cure.

Every waking minute of these nerve-shocked men was filled with activity—usually outdoor activity, such as fishing, hunting, playing ball, golf, taking pictures, making gardens, and dancing. They were given no time for brooding over their terrible experiences.

"Occupational therapy" is the term now used by psychiatry when work is prescribed as though it were a medicine. It is not new. The old Greek physicians were advocating it five hundred years before Christ was born!

Any psychiatrist will tell you that work—keeping busy—is one of the best anesthetics ever known for sick nerves. Henry W. Longfellow found that out for himself when he lost his young wife. His wife had been melting some sealing wax at a candle one day, when her clothes caught on fire. Longfellow heard her cries and tried to reach her in time; but she died from the burns. For a while, Longfellow was so tortured by the memory of that dreadful experience that he nearly went insane; but, fortunately for him, his three small children needed his attention. In spite of his own grief, Longfellow undertook to be father and mother to his children. He took them for walks, told them stories, played games with them, and immortalized their companionship in his poem *The Children's Hour*. He also translated Dante; and all these duties combined kept him so busy that he forgot himself entirely, and regained his peace of mind. As Tennyson declared when he lost his most intimate friend, Arthur Hallam, "I must lose myself in action, lest I wither in despair."

Most of us have little trouble "losing ourselves in action" while we have our noses to the grindstone and are doing our day's work. But the hours after work—they are the dangerous ones. Just when we're free to enjoy our own leisure, and ought to be happiest— that's when the blue devils of worry attack us. That's when we begin to wonder whether we're getting anywhere in life; whether we're in a rut; whether the boss "meant anything" by that remark he made today; or whether we're getting bald.

When we are not busy, our minds tend to become a near-vacuum. Every student of physics knows that "nature abhors a vacuum."

So nature rushes in to fill the vacant mind. With what? Usually with emotions. Why? Because emotions of worry, fear, hate, jealousy, and envy are driven by primeval vigor and the dynamic energy of the jungle. Such emotions are so violent that they tend to drive out of our minds all peaceful, happy thoughts and emotions.

James L. Mursell, professor of education, Teachers College, Columbia, puts it very well when he says: "Worry is most apt to ride you ragged not when you are in action, but when the day's work is done. Your imagination can run riot then and bring up all sorts of ridiculous possibilities and magnify each little blunder. At such a time," he continues, "your mind is like a motor

15

operating without its load. It races and threatens to burn out its bearings or even to tear itself to bits. The remedy for worry is to get completely occupied doing something constructive."

HOW A CHICAGO WOMAN CONQUERED WORRY

But you don't have to be a college professor to realize this truth and put it into practice. During the war, I met a housewife from Chicago who told me how she discovered for herself that "the remedy for worry is to get completely occupied doing something constructive." I met this woman and her husband in the dining car while I was traveling from New York to my farm in Missouri. (Sorry I didn't get their names—I never like to give examples without using names and street addresses—details that give authenticity to a story.)

This couple told me that their son had joined the armed forces the day after Pearl Harbor. The woman told me that she had almost wrecked her health worrying over that only son. Where was he? Was he safe? Or in action? Would he be wounded? Killed?

When I asked her how she overcame her worry, she replied: "I got busy." She told me that at first she had dismissed her maid and tried to keep busy by doing all her housework herself. But that didn't help much. "The trouble was," she said, "that I could do my housework almost mechanically, without using my mind. So I kept on worrying. While making the beds and washing the dishes I realized I needed some new kind of work that would keep me busy both mentally and physically every hour of the day. So I took a job as a saleswoman in a large department store.

"That did it," she said. "I immediately found myself in a whirlwind of activity: customers swarming around me, asking for prices, sizes, colors. Never a second to think of anything except my immediate duty; and when night came, I could think of nothing except getting off my aching feet. As soon as I ate dinner, I fell into bed and instantly became unconscious. I had neither the time nor the energy to worry."

She discovered for herself what John Cowper Powys meant when he said, in *The Art of Forgetting the Unpleasant:* "A certain comfortable security, a certain profound inner peace, a kind of happy numbness, soothes the nerves of the human animal when absorbed in its allotted task."

If you and I are worried, let's remember that we can use good old-fashioned work as a medicine. That was said by no less an authority than the late Dr. Richard C. Cabot, formerly professor of clinical medicine at Harvard. In his book *What Men Live By,* Dr. Cabot says, "As a physician, I have had the happiness of seeing work cure many persons who have suffered from trembling palsy of the soul which results from overmastering doubts, hesitations, vacillation and fear. . . . Courage given us by our work is like the self-reliance which Emerson has made forever glorious."

If you and I don't keep busy—if we sit around and brood—we will hatch out a whole flock of what Charles Darwin used to call the "wibber gibbers." And the "wibber gibbers" are nothing but old-fashioned gremlins that will run us hollow and destroy our power of action and our power of will.

George Bernard Shaw was right. He summed it all up when he said: *"The secret of being miserable is to have the leisure to bother about whether you are happy or not."* So don't bother to think about it! Spit on your hands and get busy. Your blood will start circulating; your mind will start ticking—and pretty soon this whole positive upsurge of life in your body will drive worry from your mind. *Get* busy. *Keep* busy. It's the cheapest kind of medicine there is on this earth—and one of the best.

To break the worry habit, here is **Rule 4:**

Keep busy. The worried person must lose himself in action, lest he wither in despair.

Don't Let the Beetles Get You Down

WE OFTEN face the major disasters of life bravely—and then let the trifles, the "pains in the neck," get us down. For example, Samuel Pepys tells in his *Diary* about seeing Sir Harry Vane's head chopped off in London. As Sir Harry mounted the platform, he was not pleading for his life, but was pleading with the executioner not to hit the painful boil on his neck!

Admiral Byrd discovered down in the terrible cold and darkness of the polar nights that his men fussed more about the "pains in the neck" than about the big things. They bore, without complaining, the dangers, the hardships, and the cold that was often eighty degrees below zero. "But," says Admiral Byrd, "I know of bunkmates who quit speaking because each suspected the other of inching his gear into the other's allotted space; and I knew of one who could not eat unless he could find a place in the mess hall out of sight of the Fletcherist who solemnly chewed his food twenty-eight times before swallowing.

"In a polar camp," says Admiral Byrd, "little things like that have the power to drive even disciplined men to the edge of insanity."

And you might have added, Admiral Byrd, that "little things" in marriage drive people to the edge of insanity and cause "half the heartaches in the world."

TRIVIALITIES WRECK MARRIAGES

At least, that is what the authorities say. For example, Judge Joseph Sabath of Chicago, after acting as arbiter in more than forty thousand unhappy marriages, declared: "Trivialities are at the bottom of most marital unhappiness"; and Frank S. Hogan, District Attorney of New York County, says, "Fully half the cases in our criminal courts originate in little things. Barroom bravado, domestic wrangling, an insulting remark, a disparaging word, a rude action—those are the little things that lead to assault and murder. Very few of us are cruelly and greatly wronged. It is the small blows to our self-esteem, the indignities, the little jolts to our vanity, which cause half the heartaches in the world."

When Eleanor Roosevelt was first married, she "worried for days" because her new cook had served a poor meal. "But if that happened now," Mrs. Roosevelt says, "I would shrug my shoulders and forget it." Good. That is acting like an adult emotionally. Even Catherine the Great, an absolute autocrat, used to laugh the thing off when the cook spoiled a meal.

Mrs. Carnegie and I had dinner at a friend's house in Chicago. While carving the meat, he did something wrong. I didn't notice it; and I wouldn't have cared even if I had noticed it. But his wife saw it and jumped down his throat right in front of us. "John," she cried, "watch what you are doing! Can't you ever learn to serve properly!"

Then she said to us: "He is always making mistakes. He just doesn't try." Maybe he didn't try to carve; but I certainly give him credit for trying to live with her for twenty years. Frankly, I would rather have eaten a couple of hot dogs with mustard—in an atmosphere of peace—than to have dined on Peking duck and shark fins while listening to her scolding.

Shortly after that experience, Mrs. Carnegie and I had some friends at our home for dinner. Just before they arrived, Mrs. Carnegie found that three of the napkins didn't match the tablecloth.

"I rushed to the cook," she told me later, "and found that the other three napkins had gone to the laundry. The guests were at the door. There was no time to change. I felt like bursting into tears! All I could think was, 'Why did this stupid mistake have to spoil my whole evening?' Then I thought—well—why let it? I went in to dinner, determined to have a good time. And I did. I would much rather our friends think I was a sloppy housekeeper," she told me, "than a nervous, bad-tempered one. And anyhow, as far as I could make out, no one noticed the napkins!"

A well-known legal maxim says: *De minimis non curat lex*—"the law does not concern itself with trifles." And neither should the worrier—if he wants peace of mind.

Much of the time, all we need to overcome the annoyance of trifles is to effect a shifting of emphasis—set up a new, and pleasurable, point of view in the mind. My friend Homer Croy, who wrote *They Had to See Paris* and a dozen other books, gives a wonderful example of how this can be done. He used to be driven half crazy, while working on a book, by the rattling of the radiators in his New York apartment. The steam would bang and sizzle—and he would sizzle with irritation as he sat at his desk.

"Then," says Homer Croy, "I went with some friends on a camping expedition. While listening to the limbs crackling in the roaring fire, I thought how much they sounded like the cracking of the radiators. Why should I like one and hate the other? When I went home I said to myself, 'The crackling of the limbs in the fire was a pleasant sound; the sound of the radiators is about the same—I'll go to sleep and not worry about the noise.' *And I did.* For a few days I was conscious of the radiators; but soon I forgot all about them.

"And so it is with many petty worries. We dislike them and get into a stew, all because we exaggerate their importance. . . ."

Disraeli said: "Life is too short to be little." "Those words," said André Maurois in *This Week* magazine, "have helped me through many a painful experience: often we allow ourselves to be upset by small things we should despise and forget. . . . Here we are on this earth, with only a few more decades to live, and we lose many irreplaceable hours brooding over grievances that, in a year's time, will be forgotten by us and by everybody. No, let us devote our life to worth-while actions and feelings, to great thoughts, real affections and enduring undertakings. For life is too short to be little."

Here is one of the most interesting stories that Dr. Harry Emerson Fosdick ever told—a story about the battles won and lost by a giant of the forest:

On the slope of Long's Peak in Colorado lies the ruin of a gigantic tree. Naturalists tell us that it stood for some four hundred years. It was a seedling when Columbus landed at San Salvador, and half grown when the Pilgrims settled at Plymouth. During the course of its long life it was struck by lightning fourteen times, and the innumerable avalanches and storms of four centuries thundered past it. It survived them all. In the end, however, an army of beetles attacked the tree and leveled it to the ground. The insects ate their way through the bark and gradually destroyed the inner strength of the tree by their tiny but incessant attacks. A forest giant which age had not withered, nor lightning blasted, nor storms subdued, fell at last before beetles so small that a man could crush them between his forefinger and his thumb.

Aren't we all like that battling giant of the forest? Don't we manage somehow to survive the rare storms and avalanches and lightning blasts of life, only to let our hearts be eaten out by little beetles of worry—little beetles that could be crushed between a finger and a thumb?

19

A few years ago, I traveled through the Teton National Park, in Wyoming, with Charles Seifred, highway superintendent for the state of Wyoming, and some of his friends. We were all going to visit the John D. Rockefeller estate in the park. But the car in which I was riding took the wrong turn, got lost, and drove up to the entrance of the estate an hour after the other cars had gone in. Mr. Seifred had the key that unlocked the private gate, so he waited in the hot, mosquito-infested woods for an hour until we arrived. The mosquitoes were enough to drive a saint insane. But they couldn't triumph over Charles Seifred. While waiting for us, he cut a limb off an aspen tree—and made a whistle of it. When we arrived, was he cussing the mosquitoes? No, he was playing his whistle. I have kept that whistle as a memento of a man who knew how to put trifles in their place.

Here is **Rule 5:**

Let's not allow ourselves to be upset by small things we should despise and forget. Remember "Life is too short to be little."

A Law That Will Outlaw Many of Your Worries

As a child, I grew up on a Missouri farm; and one day, while helping my mother pit cherries, I began to cry. My mother said, "Dale, what in the world are you crying about?" I blubbered, "I'm afraid I am going to be buried alive!"

I was full of worries in those days. When thunderstorms came, I worried for fear I would be killed by lightning. When hard times came, I worried for fear we wouldn't have enough to eat. I worried for fear I would go to hell when I died. I was terrified for fear an older boy, Sam White, would cut off my big ears—as he threatened to do. I worried for fear girls would laugh at me if I tipped my hat to them. I worried for fear no girl would ever be willing to marry me. I worried about what I would say to my wife immediately after we were married. I imagined that we would be married in some country church, and then get in a surrey with fringe on the top and ride back to the farm . . . but how would I be able to keep the conversation going on that ride back to the farm? How? How? I pondered over that earth-shaking problem for many an hour as I walked behind the plow.

As the years went by, I gradually discovered that ninety-nine per cent of the things I worried about never happened.

For example, as I have already said, I was once terrified of lightning; but I now know that the chances of my being killed by lightning in any one year are, according to the National Safety Council, only one in three hundred and fifty thousand.

My fear of being buried alive was even more absurd: I don't imagine that—even back in the days before embalming was the rule—one person in ten million was buried alive; yet I once cried for fear of it.

One person out of every eight dies of cancer. If I had wanted something to worry about, I should have worried about cancer—instead of being killed by lightning or being buried alive.

To be sure, I have been talking about the worries of youth and adolescence. But many of our adult worries are almost as absurd. You and I could probably eliminate nine tenths of our worries right now if we would cease our fretting long enough to discover whether, *by the law of averages,* there was any real justification for our worries.

The most famous insurance company on earth—Lloyd's of London—has made countless millions of dollars out of the tendency of everybody to worry about things that rarely happen. Lloyd's of London bets people that the disasters they are worrying about will never occur. However, *they don't call it betting. They call it insurance. But it is really betting based on the law of averages.* This great insurance firm has been going strong for two hundred years; and unless human nature changes, it will still be going strong fifty centuries from now by insuring shoes and ships and sealing wax against disasters that, *by the law of averages,* don't happen nearly so often as people imagine.

LET THE LAW OF AVERAGES WORK FOR YOU

If we examine the law of averages, we will often be astounded at the facts we uncover. For example, if I knew that during the next five years I would have to fight in a battle as bloody as the Battle of Gettysburg, I would be terrified. I would take out all the life insurance I could get. I would draw up my will and set all my earthly affairs in order. I would say, "I'll probably never live through that battle, so I had better make the most of the few years I have left." Yet the facts are that, according to the law of averages, it is just as dangerous, just as fatal, to try to live from age fifty to age fifty-five in peacetime as it was to fight in the Battle of Gettysburg. What I am trying to say is this: in times of peace, just as many people die per thousand between the ages of fifty and fifty-five as were killed per thousand among the 163,000 soldiers who fought at Gettysburg.

I wrote several chapters of this book at James Simpson's Num-Ti-Gah Lodge, on the shore of Bow Lake in the Canadian Rockies. While stopping there one summer, I met Mr. and Mrs. Herbert H. Salinger, of 2298 Pacific Avenue, San Francisco. Mrs. Salinger, a poised, serene woman, gave me the impression that she had never worried. One evening in front of the roaring fireplace, I asked her if she had ever been troubled by worry. "Troubled by it?" she said. "My life was almost *ruined* by it. Before I learned to conquer worry, I lived through eleven years of self-made hell. I was irritable and hot-tempered. I lived under terrific tension. I would take the bus every week from my home in San Mateo to shop in San Francisco. But even while shopping, I worried myself into a dither: maybe I had left the electric iron connected on the ironing board. Maybe the house had caught fire. Maybe the maid had run off and left the children. Maybe they had been out on their bicycles and been killed by a car. In the midst of my shopping, I would often worry myself into a cold perspiration and rush out and take the bus home to see if everything was all right. No wonder my first marriage ended in disaster.

"My second husband is a lawyer—a quiet, analytical man who never worries about anything. When I became tense and anxious, he would say to me, 'Relax. Let's think this out. . . . What are you really worrying about? Let's examine the law of averages and see whether or not it is likely to happen.'

"For example, I remember the time we were driving from Albuquerque, New Mexico, to the Carlsbad Caverns—driving on a dirt road—when we were caught in a terrible rainstorm.

"The car was slithering and sliding. We couldn't control it. I was positive we would slide off into one of the ditches that flanked the road; but my husband kept repeating to me: 'I am driving very slowly. Nothing serious is likely to happen. Even if the car does slide into the ditch, by the law of averages, we won't be hurt.' His calmness and confidence quieted me.

"One summer we were on a camping trip in the Touquin Valley of the Canadian Rockies. One night, we were camping seven thousand feet above sea level, when a storm threatened to tear our tents to shreds. The tents were tied with guy ropes to a wooden platform. The outer tent shook and trembled and screamed and shrieked in the wind. I expected every minute to see our tent torn loose and hurled through the sky. I was terrified! But my husband kept saying: 'Look, my dear, we are traveling with Brewsters' guides. Brewsters know what they are doing. They have been pitching tents in these mountains for sixty years. This tent has been here for many seasons. It hasn't blown down yet and, by the law of averages, it won't blow away tonight: and even if it does, we can take shelter in another tent. So relax. . . . I did; and I slept soundly the balance of the night.

"A few years ago an infantile-paralysis epidemic swept over our part of California. In the old days, I would have been hysterical. But my husband persuaded me to act calmly. We took all the precautions we could: we kept our children away from crowds, away from school and the movies. By consulting the Board of Health, we found out that even during the worst infantile-paralysis epidemic that California had ever known up to that time, only 1835 children had been stricken in the entire state of California. And that the usual number was around two hundred or three hundred. Tragic as those figures are, we nevertheless felt that, according to the law of averages, the chances of any one child being stricken were remote.

" 'By the law of averages, it won't happen.' That phrase has destroyed ninety per cent of my worries; and it has made the past twenty years of my life beautiful and peaceful beyond my highest expectations."

General George Crook—probably the greatest Indian fighter in American history—says on page 77 of his *Autobiography* that "nearly all the worries and unhappiness" of the Indians "came from their imagination, and not from reality."

As I look back across the decades, I can see that that is where most of my worries came from also. Jim Grant told me that that had been his experience, too. He owns the James A. Grant Distributing Company, 204 Franklin Street, New York City. He orders from ten to fifteen carloads of Florida oranges and grapefruit at a time. He told me that he used to torture himself with such thoughts as: What if there's a train wreck? What if my fruit is strewn all over the countryside? What if a bridge collapses as my cars are going across it? Of course, the fruit was insured; but he feared that if he didn't deliver his fruit on time, he might risk the loss of his market. He worried so much that he feared he had stomach ulcers and went to a doctor. The doctor told him there was nothing wrong with him except jumpy nerves. "I saw the light then," he said, "and began to ask myself questions. I said to myself: 'Look here, Jim Grant, how many fruit cars have you handled over the years?' The answer was: 'About twenty-five thousand.' Then I asked myself: 'How many of those cars were ever wrecked?' The answer was: 'Oh—maybe five.' Then I said to myself: 'Only five—out of twenty-five thousand? Do you know what that means? A ratio of five thousand to one! In other words, by the law of averages, based on experience, the chances are five thousand to one against one of your cars ever being wrecked. So what are you worried about?' "

"Then I said to myself: 'Well, a bridge may collapse!' Then I asked myself: 'How many cars have you actually lost from a bridge collapsing?' The answer was—'None.' Then I said to myself: 'Aren't you a fool to be worrying yourself into stomach ulcers over a bridge which has never yet collapsed, and over a railroad wreck when the chances are five thousand to one against it!' "

"When I looked at it that way," Jim Grant told me, "I felt pretty silly. I decided then and there to let the law of averages do the worrying for me—and I have not been troubled with my 'stomach ulcer' since!"

When Al Smith was Governor of New York, I heard him answer the attacks of his political enemies by saying over and over: "Let's examine the record . . . let's examine the record." Then he proceeded to give the facts. The next time you and I are worrying about what may happen, let's take a tip from wise old Al Smith: let's examine the record and see what basis there is, if any, for our gnawing anxieties.

Here is Rule 6: "Let's examine the record." Let's ask ourselves: "What are the chances, according to the law of averages, that this event I am worrying about will ever occur?"

Co-operate with the Inevitable

WHEN I WAS a little boy, I was playing with some of my friends in the attic of an old, abandoned log house in northwest Missouri. As I climbed down out of the attic, I rested my feet on a window sill for a moment—and then jumped. I had a ring on my left forefinger; and as I jumped, the ring caught on a nail-head and tore off my finger.

I screamed. I was terrified. I was positive I was going to die. But after the hand healed, I never worried about it for one split second. What would have been the use? . . . I accepted the inevitable.

Now I often go for a month at a time without even thinking about the fact that I have only three fingers and a thumb on my left hand.

It is astonishing how quickly we can accept almost any situation—if we have to—and adjust ourselves to it and forget about it.

I often think of an inscription on the ruins of a fifteenth-century cathedral in Amsterdam, Holland. This inscription says in Flemish: "It is so. It cannot be otherwise."

As you and I march across the decades of time, we are going to meet a lot of unpleasant situations that are so. They cannot be otherwise. We have our choice. We can either accept them as inevitable and adjust ourselves to them, or we can ruin our lives with rebellion and maybe end up with a nervous breakdown.

Here is a bit of sage advice from one of my favorite philosophers, William James. *"Be willing to have it so,"* he said. *"Acceptance of what has happened is the first step to overcoming the consequences of any misfortune."* Elizabeth Connley, of 2840 NE 49th Avenue, Portland, Oregon, had to find that out the hard way. Here is a letter that she wrote me recently: "On the very day that America was celebrating the victory of our armed forces in North Africa," the letter says, "I received a telegram from the War Department: my nephew —the person I loved most—was missing in action. A short time later, another telegram arrived saying he was dead.

"I was prostrate with grief. Up to that time, I had felt that life had been very good to me. I had a job I loved. I had helped to raise this nephew. He represented to me all that was fine and good in young manhood. I had felt that all the bread I had cast upon the waters was coming back to me as cake! . . . Then came this telegram. My whole world collapsed. I felt there was nothing left to live for. I neglected my work; neglected my friends. I let everything go. I was bitter and resentful. Why did my loving nephew have to be taken? Why did this good boy—with life all before him—why did he have to be killed? I couldn't accept it. My grief was so overwhelming that I decided to give up my work, and go away and hide myself in my tears and bitterness.

"I was clearing out my desk, getting ready to quit, when I came across a letter that I had forgotten—a letter from this nephew who had been killed, a letter he had written to me when my mother had died a few years ago. 'Of course, we will all miss her,' the letter said, 'and especially you. But I know you'll carry on. Your own personal philosophy will make you do that. I shall never forget the beautiful truths you taught me. Wherever I am, or how far apart we may be, I shall always remember that you taught me to smile, and to take whatever comes, like a man.'

"I read and reread that letter. It seemed as if he were there beside me, speaking to me. He seemed to be saying to me: 'Why don't you do what you taught me to do? Carry on, no matter what happens. Hide your private sorrows under a smile and carry on.'

"So, I went back to my work. I stopped being bitter and rebellious. I kept saying to myself: 'It is done. I can't change it. But I can and will carry on as he wished me to do.' I threw all my mind and strength into my work. I wrote letters to soldiers—to other people's boys. I joined an adult-education class at night—seeking out new interests and making new friends. I can hardly believe the change that has come over me. I have ceased mourning over the past that is forever gone. I am living each day now with joy—just as my nephew would have wanted me to do. I have made peace with life. I have accepted my fate. I am now living a fuller and more complete life than I have ever known."

Elizabeth Connley, out in Portland, Oregon, learned what all of us will have to learn sooner or later: namely, that we must accept and co-operate with the inevitable. "It is so. It cannot be otherwise." That is not an easy lesson to learn. Even kings on their thrones have to keep reminding themselves of it. The late George V had these framed words hanging on the wall of his library in Buckingham Palace: "Teach me neither to cry for the moon nor over spilt milk." The same thought is expressed by Schopenhauer in this way: "A good supply of resignation is of the first importance in providing for the journey of life."

Obviously, circumstances alone do not make us happy or unhappy. It is the way we react to circumstances that determines our feelings. Jesus said that the kingdom of heaven is within you. That is where the kingdom of hell is, too.

We can all endure disaster and tragedy and triumph over them—if we have to. We may not think we can, but we have surprisingly strong inner resources that will see us through if we will only make use of them. We are stronger than we think.

The late Booth Tarkington always said: "I could take anything that life could force upon me except one thing: blindness. I could never endure that."

Then one day, when he was along in his sixties, Tarkington glanced down at the carpet on the floor. The colors were blurred. He couldn't see the pattern. He went to a specialist. He learned the tragic truth: he was losing his sight. One eye was nearly blind; the other would follow. That which he feared most had come upon him.

And how did Tarkington react to this "worst of all disasters"? Did he feel, "This is *it!* This is the end of my life"? No, to his amazement, he felt quite gay. He even called upon his humor. Floating "specks" annoyed him; they would swim across his eyes and cut off his vision. Yet when the largest of these specks would swim across his sight, he would say, "Hello! There's Grandfather again! Wonder where he's going on this fine morning!"

How could fate ever conquer a spirit like that? The answer is it couldn't. When total darkness closed in, Tarkington said, "I found I could take the loss of my eyesight, just as a man can take anything else. If I lost *all five* of my senses, I know I could live on inside my mind. For it is in the mind we see, and in the mind we live, whether we know it or not."

In the hope of restoring his eyesight, Tarkington had to go through more than twelve operations within one year. With *local* anesthetic! Did he rail against this? He knew it had to be done. He knew he couldn't escape it, so the only way to lessen his suffering was to take it with grace. He refused a private room at the hospital and went into a ward, where he could be with other people who had troubles, too. He tried to cheer them up. And when he had to submit to repeated operations—fully conscious of what was being done to his eyes—he tried to remember how fortunate he was. "How wonderful!" he said. "How wonderful, that science now has the skill to operate on anything so delicate as the human eye!"

The average man would have been a nervous wreck if he had had to endure more than twelve operations and blindness. Yet Tarkington said, "I would not exchange this experience for a happier one." It taught him acceptance. It taught him that nothing life could bring him was beyond his strength to endure. It taught him, as John Milton discovered, that "It is not miserable to be blind, it is only miserable not to be able to endure blindness."

Margaret Fuller, the famous New England feminist, once offered as her credo: "I accept the Universe!"

When grouchy old Thomas Carlyle heard that in England, he snorted, "By gad, she'd better!" Yes, and by gad, you and I had better accept the inevitable, too!

If we rail and kick against it and grow bitter, we won't change the inevitable; but we will change ourselves. I know. I have tried it.

I once refused to accept an inevitable situation with which I was confronted. I played the fool and railed against it, and rebelled. I turned my nights into hells of insomnia. I brought upon myself everything I didn't want. Finally, after a year of self-torture, I had to accept what I knew from the outset I couldn't possibly alter.

I should have cried out years ago with old Walt Whitman:

> Oh, to confront night, storms, hunger,
> Ridicule, accident, rebuffs as the trees
> and animals do.

I spent twelve years working with cattle; yet I never saw a Jersey cow running a temperature because the pasture was burning up from a lack of rain or because of sleet and cold or because her boy friend was paying too much attention to another heifer. The animals confront night, storms, and hunger calmly; so they never have nervous breakdowns or stomach ulcers; and they never go insane.

Am I advocating that we simply bow down to *all* the adversities that come our way? Not by a long shot! That is mere fatalism. As long as there is a chance that we can save a situation, let's fight! But when common sense tells us that we are up against something that is so—and cannot be otherwise—then, in the name of our sanity, let's not look before and after and pine for what is not.

The late Dean Hawkes of Columbia University told me that he had taken a Mother Goose rhyme as one of his mottoes:

> For every ailment under the sun,
> There is a remedy, or there is none;
> If there be one, try to find it;
> If there be none, never mind it.

While writing this book, I interviewed a number of the leading businessmen of America; and I was impressed by the fact that they co-operated with the inevitable and led lives singularly free from worry. If they hadn't done that, they would have cracked under the strain. Here are a few examples of what I mean:

J. C. Penney, founder of the nation-wide chain of Penney stores, said to me: "I wouldn't worry if I lost every dollar I have because I don't see what is to be gained by worrying. I do the best job I possibly can; and leave the results in the laps of the gods."

Henry Ford told me much the same thing. "When I can't handle events," he said, "I let them handle themselves."

When I asked K. T. Keller, president of the Chrysler Corporation, how he kept from worrying, he replied: "When I am up against a tough situation, if I can do anything about it, I do it. If I can't, I just forget it. I never worry about the future, because I know no man living can possibly figure out what is going to happen in the future. There are so many forces that will affect that future! Nobody can tell what prompts those forces—or understand them. So why worry about them?" K. T. Keller would be embarrassed if you told him he is a philosopher. He is just a good businessman, yet he has stumbled on the same philosophy that Epictetus taught in Rome nineteen centuries ago. "There is only one way to happiness," Epictetus taught the Romans, "and that is to cease worrying about things which are beyond the power of our will."

Why do you think your automobile tires stand up on the road and take so much punishment? At first, the tire manufacturers tried to make a tire that would resist the shocks of the road. It was soon cut to ribbons. Then they made a tire that would absorb the shocks of the road. That tire could "take it." You and I will last longer, and enjoy smoother riding, if we learn to absorb the shocks and jolts along the rocky road of life.

During the past eight years, I have been reading practically every book and magazine article I could find that dealt even remotely with banishing worry. . . . Would you like to know what is the best single bit of advice about worry that I have ever discovered in all that reading? Well, here it is—summed up in twenty-seven words—words that you and I ought to paste on our bathroom mirrors, so that each time we wash our faces we could also wash away all worry from our minds. This priceless prayer was written by Dr. Reinhold Niebuhr, Professor of Applied Christianity, Union Theological Seminary, Broadway at 120th Street, New York.

> *God grant me the serenity*
> *To accept the things I cannot change;*
> *The courage to change the things I can;*
> *And the wisdom to know the difference.*

To break the worry habit, **Rule 7** is: **Co-operate with the inevitable.**

Eight Words That Can Transform Your Life

A FEW YEARS AGO, I was asked to answer this question on a radio program: "What is the biggest lesson you have ever learned?"

That was easy: by far the most vital lesson I have ever learned is the importance of what we think. If I knew what you think, I would know what you are. Our thoughts make us what we are. Our mental attitude is the X factor that determines our fate. Emerson said: "A man is what he thinks about all day long." . . . How could he possibly be anything else?

I now know with a conviction beyond all doubt that the biggest problem you and I have to deal with—in fact, almost the *only* problem we have to deal with—is choosing the right thoughts. If we can do that, we will be on the highroad to solving all our problems. The great philosopher who ruled the Roman Empire, Marcus Aurelius, summed it up in eight words—*eight words that can determine your destiny: "Our life is what our thoughts make it."*

Yes, if we think happy thoughts, we will be happy. If we think miserable thoughts, we will be miserable. If we think fear thoughts, we will be fearful. If we think sickly thoughts, we will probably be ill. If we think failure, we will certainly fail. If we wallow in self-pity, everyone will want to shun us and avoid us. "You are not," said Norman Vincent Peale, "you are not what you think you are; but what you *think*, you are."

What do I mean? Have I the colossal effrontery to tell you to your face—when you are mowed down by troubles, and your nerves are sticking out like wires and curling up at the ends—have I the colossal effrontery to tell you that, under those conditions, you can change your mental attitude by an effort of the will? Yes, I mean precisely that! And that is not all. I am going to show you *how* to do it. It may take a little effort, but the secret is simple.

William James, who has never been topped in his knowledge of practical psychology, once made this observation: "*Action seems to follow feeling, but really action and feeling go together; and by regulating the action, which is under the more direct control of the will, we can indirectly regulate the feeling, which is not.*"

In other words, William James tells us that we cannot instantly change our emotions just by "making up our minds to"—but that we *can* change our actions. And that when we change our actions, we will automatically change our feelings.

"*Thus,*" he explains, "*the sovereign voluntary path to cheerfulness, if your cheerfulness be lost, is to sit up cheerfully and to act and speak as if cheerfulness were already there.*"

Does that simple trick work? It works like plastic surgery! Try it yourself. Put a big, broad, honest-to-God smile on your face; throw back your shoulders; take a good, deep breath; and sing a snatch of song. If you can't sing, whistle. If you can't whistle, hum. You will quickly discover what William James was talking about—that it is *physically impossible* to remain blue or depressed while you are acting out the symptoms of being radiantly happy!

This is one of the little basic truths of nature that can easily work miracles in all of our lives. I know a woman in California—I won't mention her name—who could wipe out all of her miseries in twenty-four hours if only she knew this secret. She's old, and she's a widow—that's sad, I admit—but does she try to act happy? No; if you ask her how she is feeling, she says, "Oh, I'm all right"—but the expression on her face and the whine in her voice say, "Oh, God, if you only knew the troubles I've seen!" She seems to reproach you for being happy in her presence. Hundreds of women are worse off than she is: her husband left her enough insurance to last the rest of her life, and she has married children to give her a home. But I've rarely seen her smile. She complains that all three of her sons-in-law are stingy and selfish—although she is a guest in their homes for months at a time. And she complains that her daughters never give her presents—although she hoards her own money carefully, "for my old age." She is a blight on herself and her unfortunate family! But does it have to be so? That is the pity of it—she could change herself from a miserable, bitter, and unhappy old woman into an honored and beloved member of the family—if she *wanted* to change. And all she would have to do to work this transformation would be to start acting cheerful; start acting as though she had a little love to give away—instead of squandering it all on her own unhappy and embittered self.

I know a man in Indiana—H. J. Englert, of 1335 11th Street, Tell City, Indiana—who is still alive today because he discovered this secret. Ten years ago Mr. Englert had a case of scarlet fever; and when he recovered, he found he had developed nephritis, a kidney disease. He tried all kinds of doctors, "even quacks," he informs me, but nothing could cure him.

Then, a short time ago, he got other complications. His blood pressure soared. He went to a doctor, and was told that his blood pressure was hitting the top at 214. He was told that it was fatal—that the condition was progressive, and he had better put his affairs in order at once.

"I went home," he says, "and made sure that my insurance was all paid up, then I apologized to my Maker for all my mistakes, and settled down to gloomy meditations. I made everyone unhappy. My wife and family were miserable, and I was buried deep in depression myself. However, after a week of wallowing in self-pity, I said to myself, 'You're acting like a fool! You may not die for a year yet, so why not try to be happy while you're here?'

"I threw back my shoulders, put a smile on my face, and attempted to act as though everything were normal. I admit it was an effort at first—but I forced myself to be pleasant and cheerful; and this not only helped my family, but it also helped me.

"The first thing I knew, I began to *feel* better—almost as well as I pretended to feel! The improvement went on. And today—months after I was supposed

30

to be in my grave—I am not only happy, well, and alive, but my blood pressure is down! I know one thing for certain: the doctor's prediction would certainly have come true if I had gone on thinking 'dying' thoughts of defeat. But I gave my body a chance to heal itself, by nothing in the world but a change of mental attitude!"

Let me ask you a question: If merely acting cheerful and thinking positive thoughts of health and courage could save this man's life, why should you and I tolerate for one minute more our minor glooms and depressions? Why make ourselves, and everyone around us, unhappy and blue, when it is possible for us to start creating happiness by merely acting cheerful?

According to the book of Genesis, the Creator gave man dominion over the whole wide earth. A mighty big present. But I am not interested in any such superroyal prerogatives. All I desire is dominion over myself—dominion over my thoughts; dominion over my fears; dominion over my mind and over my spirit. And the wonderful thing is that I know that I can attain this dominion to an astonishing degree, any time I want to, by merely controlling my actions —which in turn control my reactions.

So let us remember these words of William James: *"Much of what we call Evil . . . can often be converted into a bracing and tonic good by a simple change of the sufferer's inner attitude from one of fear to one of fight."*

Let's *fight* for our happiness!

Let's fight for our happiness by following a daily program of cheerful and constructive thinking. Here is such a program. It is entitled "Just for Today." I found this program so inspiring that I gave away hundreds of copies. It was written thirty-six years ago by the late Sibyl F. Partridge. If you and I follow it, we will eliminate most of our worries and increase immeasurably our portion of what the French call *la joie de vivre*.

JUST FOR TODAY

1. Just for today I will be happy. This assumes that what Abraham Lincoln said is true, that "most folks are about as happy as they make up their minds to be." Happiness is from within; it is not a matter of externals.

2. Just for today I will try to adjust myself to what is, and not try to adjust everything to my own desires. I will take my family, my business, and my luck as they come and fit myself to them.

3. Just for today I will take care of my body. I will exercise it, care for it, nourish it, not abuse it nor neglect it, so that it will be a perfect machine for my bidding.

4. Just for today I will try to strengthen my mind. I will learn something useful. I will not be a mental loafer. I will read something that requires effort, thought and concentration.

5. Just for today I will exercise my soul in three ways; I will do somebody a good turn and not get found out. I will do at least two things I don't want to do, as William James suggests, just for exercise.

31

6. Just for today I will be agreeable. I will look as well as I can, dress as becomingly as possible, talk low, act courteously, be liberal with praise, criticize not at all, nor find fault with anything and not try to regulate nor improve anyone.

7. Just for today I will try to live through this day only, not to tackle my whole life problem at once. I can do things for twelve hours that would appall me if I had to keep them up for a lifetime.

8. Just for today I will have a program. I will write down what I expect to do every hour. I may not follow it exactly, but I will have it. It will eliminate two pests, hurry and indecision.

9. Just for today I will have a quiet half-hour all by myself and relax. In this half-hour sometimes I will think of God, so as to get a little more perspective into my life.

10. Just for today I will be unafraid, especially I will not be afraid to be happy, to enjoy what is beautiful, to love, and to believe that those I love, love me.

If we want to develop a mental attitude that will bring us peace and happiness, here is **Rule 8:**

Think and act cheerfully, and you will feel cheerful.

Would You Take a Million Dollars for What You Have?

SCHOPENHAUER SAID: "We seldom think of what we have but always of what we lack." Yes, the tendency to "seldom think of what we have but always of what we lack" is the greatest tragedy on earth. It has probably caused more misery than all the wars and diseases in history.

About ninety per cent of the things in our lives are right and about ten per cent are wrong. If we want to be happy, all we have to do is to concentrate on the ninety per cent that are right and ignore the ten per cent that are wrong. If we want to be worried and bitter and have stomach ulcers, all we have to do is to concentrate on the ten per cent that are wrong and ignore the ninety per cent that are glorious.

Logan Pearsall Smith packed a lot of wisdom into a few words when he said: "There are two things to aim at in life: first, to get what you want; and, after that, to enjoy it. Only the wisest of mankind achieve the second."

Would you like to know how to make even dishwashing at the kitchen sink a thrilling experience? If so, read an inspiring book of incredible courage by Borghild Dahl. It is called *I Wanted to See.* You may borrow it from your public library or purchase it from your local bookstore or from the publisher, The Macmillan Company, 60 Fifth Avenue, New York City. Price $2.25.

This book was written by a woman who was practically blind for half a century. "I had only one eye," she writes, "and it was so covered with dense scars that I had to do all my seeing through one small opening in the left of the eye. I could see a book only by holding it up close to my face and by straining my one eye as hard as I could to the left."

But she refused to be pitied, refused to be considered "different." As a child, she wanted to play hopscotch with other children, but she couldn't see the markings. So after the other children had gone home, she got down on the ground and crawled along with her eyes near to the marks. She memorized every bit of the ground where she and her friends played and soon became an expert at running games. She did her reading at home, holding a book of large print so close to her eyes that her eyelashes brushed the pages. She earned two college degrees: an A.B. from the University of Minnesota and a Master of Arts from Columbia University.

She started teaching in the tiny village of Twin Valley, Minnesota, and rose until she became professor of journalism and literature at Augustana College in Sioux Falls, South Dakota. She taught there for thirteen years, lecturing before women's clubs and giving radio talks about books and authors. "In the back of my mind," she writes, "there had always lurked a fear of total blindness. In order to overcome this, I had adopted a cheerful, almost hilarious, attitude toward life."

Then in 1943, when she was fifty-two years old, a miracle happened: an operation at the famous Mayo Clinic. She could now see forty times as well as she had ever been able to see before.

A new and exciting world of loveliness opened before her. She now found it thrilling even to wash dishes in the kitchen sink. "I begin to play with the white fluffy suds in the dishpan," she writes. "I dip my hands into them and I pick up a ball of tiny soap bubbles. I hold them up against the light, and in each of them I can see the brilliant colors of a miniature rainbow."

As she looked through the window above the kitchen sink, she saw "the flapping gray-black wings of the sparrows flying through the thick, falling snow."

She found such ecstasy looking at the soap bubbles and sparrows that she closed her book with these words: " 'Dear Lord,' I whisper, 'Our Father in Heaven, I thank Thee. I thank Thee.' "

Imagine thanking God because you can wash dishes and see rainbows in bubbles and sparrows flying through the snow!

You and I ought to be ashamed of ourselves. All the days of our years we have been living in a fairyland of beauty, but we have been too blind to see, too satiated to enjoy.

If we want to stop worrying and start living, **Rule 9** is:

Count your blessings—not your troubles!

How to Cure Melancholy in Fourteen Days

HERE IS the most astonishing statement that I ever read from the pen of a great psychiatrist. This statement was made by Alfred Adler. He used to say to his melancholia patients: "You can be cured in fourteen days if you follow this prescription. Try to think every day how you can please someone."

Dr. Adler urges us to do a good deed every day. And what is a good deed? "A good deed," said the prophet Mohammed, "is one that brings a smile of joy to the face of another."

Why will doing a good deed every day produce such astounding effects on the doer? Because trying to please others will cause us to stop thinking of ourselves: the very thing that produces worry and fear and melancholia.

Mrs. William T. Moon, who operates the Moon Secretarial School, 521 Fifth Avenue, New York, didn't have to spend two weeks thinking how she could please someone in order to banish her melancholy. She went Alfred Adler one better—no, she went Adler *thirteen* better. She banished her melancholy, not in fourteen days, but in *one* day, by thinking how she could please a couple of orphans.

It happened like this: "In December, five years ago," said Mrs. Moon, "I was engulfed in a feeling of sorrow and self-pity. After several years of happy married life, I had lost my husband. As the Christmas holidays approached, my sadness deepened. I had never spent a Christmas alone in all my life; and I dreaded to see this Christmas come. Friends had invited me to spend Christmas with them. But I did not feel up to any gaiety. I knew I would be a wet blanket at any party. So, I refused their kind invitations. As Christmas Eve approached, I was more and more overwhelmed with self-pity. True, I should have been thankful for many things, as all of us have many things for which to be thankful. The day before Christmas, I left my office at three o'clock in the afternoon and started walking aimlessly up Fifth Avenue, hoping that I might banish my self-pity and melancholy. The avenue was jammed with gay and happy crowds—scenes that brought back memories of happy years that were gone. I just couldn't bear the thought of going home to a lonely and empty apartment. I was bewildered. I didn't know what to do. I couldn't keep the tears back. After walking aimlessly for an hour or so, I found myself in front of a bus terminal. I remembered that my husband and I had often boarded an unknown bus for adventure, so I boarded the first bus I found at the station. After crossing the Hudson River and riding for some time, I heard the bus conductor say, 'Last stop, lady.' I got off. I didn't even know the name of the town. It was a quiet, peaceful little place. While waiting for the next bus home, I started walking up a residential street. As I passed a church, I heard the beautiful strains of 'Silent Night.' I went in. The church was empty except for the organist. I sat down unnoticed in one of the pews. The lights from the gaily decorated Christmas tree made the decorations seem like myriads of stars dancing in the moonbeams. The long-drawn cadences of the music—and the fact that I had forgotten to eat since morning—made me drowsy. I was weary and heavy-laden, so I drifted off to sleep.

"When I awoke, I didn't know where I was. I was terrified. I saw in front of me two small children who had apparently come in to see the Christmas tree. One, a little girl, was pointing at me and saying 'I wonder if Santa Claus brought her.' These children were also frightened when I awoke. I told them that I wouldn't hurt them. They were poorly dressed. I asked them where their mother and daddy were. 'We ain't got no mother and daddy,' they said. Here were two little orphans much worse off than I had ever been. They made me feel ashamed of my sorrow and self-pity. I showed them the Christmas tree and then took them to a drugstore and we had some refreshments, and I bought them some candy and a few presents. My loneliness vanished as if by magic. These two orphans gave me the only real happiness and self-forgetfulness that I had had in months. As I chatted with them, I realized how lucky I had been. I thanked God that all my Christmases as a child had been bright with parental love and tenderness. Those two little orphans did far more for me than I did for them. That experience showed me again the necessity of making other people happy in order to be happy ourselves. I found that happiness is contagious. By giving, we receive. By helping someone and giving out love, I had conquered worry and sorrow and self-pity, and felt like a new person. And I was a new person—not only then, but in the years that followed."

I could fill a book with stories of people who forgot themselves into health and happiness.

A Chinese proverb puts it this way: "A bit of fragrance always clings to the hand that gives you roses." However humdrum your existence may be, you surely meet *some* people every day of your life. What do you do about them? Do you merely stare through them, or do you try to find out what it is that makes them tick? How about the postman, for example—he walks hundreds of miles every year, delivering mail to your door; but have you ever taken the trouble to find out where *he* lives, or ask to see a snapshot of his wife and his kids? Did you ever ask him if his feet get tired, or if he ever gets bored?

What's in it for you? Much greater happiness! Greater satisfaction, and pride in yourself! Aristotle called this kind of attitude "enlightened selfishness." Zoroaster said, "Doing good to others is not a duty. It is a joy, for it increases your own health and happiness."

If you are a man, skip this paragraph. It won't interest you. It tells how a worried, unhappy girl got several men to propose to her. The girl who did that is a grandmother now. A few years ago, I spent the night in her and her husband's home. I had been giving a lecture in her town; and the next morning she drove me about fifty miles to catch a train on the main line of the New York Central. We got to talking about winning friends, and she said: "Mr. Carnegie, I am going to tell you something that I have never confessed to anyone before—not even to my husband." (By the way, this story isn't going to be half so interesting as you probably imagine.) She told me that she had been reared in a social-register family in Philadelphia. "The tragedy of my girlhood and young womanhood," she said, "was our poverty. We could never entertain the way the other girls in my social set entertained. My clothes were never of the best quality. I outgrew them and they didn't fit and they were often out of style. I was so humiliated, so ashamed, that I often cried myself to sleep. Finally, in sheer desperation, I hit upon the idea of always asking my partner at dinner parties to tell me about his experience, his ideas, and his plans for the future. I didn't ask these questions because I was especially interested in the answers. I did it solely to keep my partner from looking at my poor clothes. But a strange thing happened: as I listened to these young men talk and learned more about them, I really became interested in listening to what they had to say. I became so interested that I myself sometimes forgot about my clothes. But the astounding thing to me was this: since I was a good listener and encouraged the boys to talk about themselves, I gave them happiness and I gradually became the most popular girl in our social group and three of these men proposed marriage to me."

(There you are, girls: that is the way it is done.)

So if you want to increase your own health and happiness, **Rule 10** is:

Forget yourself by becoming interested in others. Do every day a good deed that will put a smile of joy on someone's face.

How the Housewife Can Avoid Fatigue—
and Keep Looking Young!

ONE DAY last autumn, my associate flew up to Boston to attend a session of one of the most unusual medical classes in the world. Medical? Well, yes. It meets once a week at the Boston Dispensary, and the patients who attend it get regular and thorough medical examinations before they are admitted. But actually this class is a psychological clinic. Although it is officially called the Class in Applied Psychology (formerly the Thought Control Class—a name suggested by the first member), its real purpose is to deal with people *who are ill from worry*. And many of these patients are emotionally disturbed housewives.

How did such a class for worriers get started? Well, in 1930, Dr. Joseph H. Pratt—who, by the way, had been a pupil of Sir William Osler—observed that many of the outpatients who came to the Boston Dispensary apparently had nothing wrong with them at all physically; yet they had practically all the symptoms that flesh is heir to. One woman's hands were so crippled with "arthritis" that she had lost all use of them. Another was in agony with all the excruciating symptoms of "cancer of the stomach." Others had backaches, headaches, were chronically tired, or had vague aches and pains. *They actually felt these pains.* But the most exhaustive medical examinations showed that nothing whatever was wrong with these women—in the physical sense. Many old-fashioned doctors would have said it was all imagination—"all in the mind."

But Dr. Pratt realized that it was no use to tell these patients to "go home and forget it." He knew that most of these women didn't want to be sick; if it was so easy to forget their ailments, they would do so themselves. So what could be done?

He opened this class—to a chorus of doubts from the medical doubters on the sidelines. And the class worked wonders! In the eighteen years that have passed since it started, thousands of patients have been "cured" by attending it. Some of the patients have been coming for years—as religious in their attendance as though going to church. My assistant talked to a woman who has hardly missed a session in more than nine years. She said that when she first went to the clinic, she was thoroughly convinced she had a floating kidney and some kind of heart ailment. She was so worried and tense that she occasionally lost her eyesight and had spells of blindness. Yet today she is confident and cheerful and in excellent health. She looked only about forty, yet she held one of her grandchildren asleep in her lap. "I used to worry so much about my family troubles," she said, "that I wished I could die. But I learned at this clinic the futility of worrying. I learned to stop it. And I can honestly say now that my life is serene."

Dr. Rose Hilferding, the medical adviser of the class, said that she thought one of the best remedies for lightening worry is "talking your troubles over with someone you trust. We call it catharsis," she said. "When patients come here, they can talk their troubles over at length, until they get them off their minds. Brooding over worries alone, and keeping them to oneself, causes great nervous tension. We all have to share our troubles. We have to share worry. We have to feel there is someone in the world who is willing to listen and able to understand."

My assistant witnessed the great relief that came to one woman from talking out her worries. She had domestic worries, and when she first began to talk, she was like a wound-up spring. Then gradually, as she kept on talking, she began to calm down. At the end of the interview, she was actually smiling. Had the problem been solved? No, it wasn't that easy. What caused the change was *talking to someone*, getting a little advice and a little human sympathy. What had really worked the change was the tremendous healing value that lies in—*words!*

Psychoanalysis is based, to some extent, on this healing power of words. Ever since the days of Freud, analysts have known that a patient could find relief from his inner anxieties if he could talk, just talk. Why is this so? Maybe because by talking, we gain a little better insight into our troubles, get a better perspective. No one knows the whole answer. But all of us know that "spitting it out" or "getting it off our chests" brings almost instant relief.

So the next time we have an emotional problem, why don't we look around for someone to talk to? I don't mean, of course, to go around making pests of ourselves by whining and complaining to everyone in sight. Let's decide on someone we can trust, and make an appointment. Maybe a relative, a doctor, a lawyer, a minister, or priest. Then say to that person: "I want your advice. I have a problem, and I wish you would listen while I put it in words. You may be able to advise me. You may see angles to this thing that I can't see myself. But even if you can't, you will help me tremendously if you will just sit and listen while I talk it out."

Talking things out, then, is one of the principal therapies used at the Boston Dispensary Class. But here are some other ideas we picked up at the class— things you, as a housewife, can do in your home.

5 RULES FOR A HAPPIER HOME LIFE

1. *Keep a notebook or scrapbook for "inspirational" reading.* Into this book you can paste all the poems, or short prayers, or quotations, which appeal to you personally and give you a lift. Then, when a rainy afternoon sends your spirits plunging down, perhaps you can find a recipe in this book for dispelling the gloom. Many patients at the Dispensary have kept such notebooks for years. They say it is a spiritual "shot in the arm."

2. *Don't dwell too long on the shortcomings of others!* Sure, your husband has faults! If he had been a saint, he never would have married you. Right? One woman at the class who found herself developing into a scolding, nagging, and haggard-faced wife, was brought up short with the question: "What would you do if your husband died?" She was so shocked by the idea that she immediately sat down and drew up a list of all her husband's good points. She made quite a list. Why don't you try the same thing the next time you feel you married a tight-fisted tyrant? Maybe you'll find, after reading his virtues, that he's a man you'd like to meet!

3. *Get interested in your neighbors!* Develop a friendly, healthy interest in the people who share the life on your street. One ailing woman who felt herself so "exclusive" that she hadn't any friends, was told to try to make up a story about the next person she met. She began, in the streetcar, to weave backgrounds and settings for the people she saw. She tried to imagine what their lives had been like. First thing you know, she was talking to people everywhere—and today she is happy, alert, and a charming human being, cured of her "pains."

4. *Make up a schedule for tomorrow's work before you go to bed tonight.* The class found that many wives feel driven and harassed by the unending round of housework and things they must do. They never got their work finished. They were chased by the clock. To cure this sense of hurry, *and* worry, the suggestion was made that they draw up a schedule each night for the following day. What happened? More work accomplished; much less fatigue; a feeling of pride and achievement; and time left over to rest and to "primp." (Every woman ought to take some time out in the course of the day to primp and look pretty. My own guess is that when a woman *knows* she looks pretty, she has little use for "nerves.")

5. *Finally—avoid tension and fatigue. Relax! Relax!* Nothing will make you look old sooner than tension and fatigue. Nothing will work such havoc with your freshness and looks!

Yes, you, as a housewife, have got to relax! You have one great advantage— you can lie down whenever you want to, and *you can lie on the floor!* Strangely enough, a good hard floor is better to relax on than an inner-spring bed. It gives more resistance. It is good for the spine.

EXERCISES THAT HELP YOU RELAX

HERE ARE some relaxing exercises you can do in your home. Try them for a week—and see what you do for your looks and disposition!

1. Lie flat on the floor whenever you feel tired. Stretch as tall as you can. Roll around if you want to. Do it twice a day.
2. Close your eyes. You might try saying something like this: "The sun is shining overhead. The sky is blue and sparkling. Nature is calm and in control of the world—and I, as nature's child, am in tune with the Universe." Or—better still —pray!
3. If you cannot lie down, because the roast is in the oven and you can't spare the time, then you can achieve almost the same effect sitting down in a chair. A hard, upright chair is the best for relaxing. Sit upright in the chair like a seated Egyptian statue, and let your hands rest, palms down, on the tops of your thighs.
4. Now, slowly tense the toes—then let them relax. Tense the muscles in your legs—and let them relax. Do this slowly upward, with all the muscles of your body, until you get to the neck. Then let your head roll around heavily, as though it were a football. Keep saying to your muscles, "Let go . . . let go. . . ."
5. Quiet your nerves with slow, steady breathing. Breathe from deep down. The yogis of India were right: rhythmical breathing is one of the best methods ever discovered for soothing the nerves.
6. Think of the wrinkles and frowns in your face, and smooth them all out. Loosen up the worry-creases you feel between your brows, and at the sides of your mouth. Do this twice a day, and maybe you won't have to go to a beauty parlor to get a massage. Maybe the lines will disappear from the inside out!

How to Keep from Worrying about Insomnia

Do YOU WORRY when you can't sleep well? Then it may interest you to know that Samuel Untermyer—the famous international lawyer—never got a decent night's sleep in his life.

When Sam Untermyer went to college, he worried about two afflictions—asthma and insomnia. He couldn't seem to cure either, so he decided to do the next best thing—take advantage of his wakefulness. Instead of tossing and turning and worrying himself into a breakdown, he would get up and study. The result? He began ticking off honors in all of his classes, and became one of the prodigies of the College of the City of New York.

Even after he started to practice law, his insomnia continued. But Untermyer didn't worry. "Nature," he said, "will take care of me." Nature did. In spite of the small amount of sleep he was getting, his health kept up and he was able to work as hard as any of the young lawyers of the New York Bar. He even worked harder, for he worked while they slept!

At the age of twenty-one, Sam Untermyer was earning seventy-five thousand dollars a year; and other young attorneys rushed to courtrooms to study his methods. In 1931, he was paid—for handling one case—what was probably the highest lawyer's fee in all history: a cool million dollars—cash on the barrelhead.

Still he had insomnia—read half the night—and then got up at five A.M. and started dictating letters. By the time most people were just starting work, *his* day's work would be almost half done. He lived to the age of eighty-one, this man who had rarely had a sound night's sleep; but if he had fretted and worried about his insomnia, he would probably have wrecked his life.

Worrying about insomnia will hurt you far more than insomnia.

Dr. Nathaniel Kleitman, professor at the University of Chicago, has done more research work on sleep than has any other living man. He is the world's expert on sleep. He declares that he has never known anyone to die from insomnia. To be sure, a man might worry about insomnia until he lowered his vitality and was swept away by germs. But it was the worry that did the damage, not the insomnia itself.

The first requisite for a good night's sleep is a feeling of security. We need to feel that some power greater than ourselves will take care of us until morning. Dr. Thomas Hyslop, of the Great West Riding Asylum, stressed that point in an address before the British Medical Association. He said: "One of the best sleep-producing agents which my years of practice have revealed to me is—*prayer*. I say this purely as a medical man. The exercise of prayer, in those who habitually exert it, must be regarded as the most adequate and normal of all the pacifiers of the mind and calmers of the nerves."

"Let God—and let go."

Jeanette MacDonald told me that when she was depressed and worried and had difficulty in going to sleep, she could always get "a feeling of security" by repeating Psalm XXIII: "The Lord is my shepherd; I shall not want. He maketh me to lie down in green pastures: he leadeth me beside the still waters. . . ."

But if you are not religious, and have to do things the hard way, then learn to relax by physical measures. Dr. David Harold Fink, who wrote *Release from Nervous Tension*, says that the best way to do this is to *talk* to your body. According to Dr. Fink, words are the key to all kinds of hypnosis; and when you consistently can't sleep, it is because you have *talked* yourself into a case of insomnia. The way to undo this is to dehypnotize yourself—and you can do it by saying to the muscles of your body, "Let go, let go—loosen up

41

and relax." We already know that the mind and nerves can't relax while the muscles are tense—so if we want to go to sleep, we start with the muscles. Dr. Fink recommends—and it works out in practice—that we put a pillow under the knees to ease the tension on the legs, and that we tuck small pillows under the arms for the very same reason. Then, by telling the jaw to relax, the eyes, the arms, and the legs, we finally drop off to sleep before we know what has hit us. I've tried it—I know. If you have trouble sleeping, get hold of Dr. Fink's book, *Release from Nervous Tension*. It is the only book I know of that is both lively reading and a cure for insomnia.

So, to keep from worrying about insomnia, here are four rules:

1. **If you can't sleep, do what Samuel Untermyer did. Get up and work or read until you do feel sleepy.**
2. **Remember that no one was ever killed by lack of sleep. Worrying about insomnia usually causes far more damage than sleeplessness.**
3. **Try prayer—or repeat Psalm XXIII, as Jeanette MacDonald does.**
4. **Relax your body. Read the book "Release from Nervous Tension."**

How to Lessen Your Financial Worries

IF I KNEW how to solve everybody's financial worries, I wouldn't be writing this book, I would be sitting in the White House—right beside the President. But here is one thing I can do: I can quote some authorities on this subject and make some highly practical suggestions and point out where you can obtain books and pamphlets that will give you additional guidance.

Seventy per cent of all our worries, according to a survey made by the *Ladies' Home Journal*, are about money. George Gallup, of the Gallup Poll, says that his research indicates that most people believe that they would have no more financial worries if they could increase their income by only ten per cent. That is true in many cases, but in a surprisingly large number of cases it is *not* true. For example, while writing this chapter, I interviewed an expert on budgets: Mrs. Elsie Stapleton—a woman who spent years as financial adviser to the customers of Wanamaker's Department Store in New York and of Gimbels. She has spent additional years as an individual consultant, trying to help people who were frantic with worry about money. She has helped people in all kinds of income brackets, all the way from a porter who earned less than a thousand dollars a year to an executive earning one hundred thousand a year. And this is what she told me: "More money is *not* the answer to most people's financial worries. In fact, I have often seen it happen that an increase in income accomplished nothing but an increase in spending—and an increase in headaches. What causes most people to worry," she said, "is not that they haven't enough money, but that *they don't know how to spend the money they have!*" . . . You snorted at that last sentence, didn't you? Well, before you snort again, please remember that Mrs. Stapleton did *not* say that was true of *all* people. She said, *"most people."* She didn't mean you. She meant your sisters and your cousins, whom you reckon by the dozens.

Leon Shimkin, general manager of the firm that publishes this book, pointed out to me a curious blindness that many people have in regard to their money. He told me about a bookkeeper he knows, a man who is a wizard at figures when working for his firm—yet when it comes to handling his personal finances! . . . Well, if this man gets paid on Friday noon, let us say, he will walk down the street, see an overcoat in a store window that strikes his fancy, and buy it—never giving a thought to the fact that rent, electric lights, and all kinds of "fixed" charges have to come out of that pay envelope sooner or later. No—he has the cash in his pocket, and that's all that counts. Yet this man knows that if the company he works for conducted its business in such a slap-happy manner, it would end up in bankruptcy.

Here's something to consider—*where your money is concerned, you're in business for yourself!* And it is literally "your business" what you do with your money.

But what are the principles of managing our money? How do we begin to make a budget and a plan? Here are nine rules.

Rule No. 1: Get the facts down on paper!

When Arnold Bennett started out in London fifty years ago to be a novelist, he was poor and hard-pressed. So he kept a record of what he did with every sixpence. Did he wonder where his money was going? No. He knew. He liked the idea so much that he continued to keep such a record even after he became rich, world-famous, and had a private yacht.

John D. Rockefeller, Sr., also kept a ledger. He knew to the penny just where he stood before he said his prayers at night and climbed into bed.

You and I, too, will have to get notebooks and start keeping records. For the rest of our lives? No, not necessarily. Experts on budgets recommend that we keep an accurate account of every nickel we spend for at least the first month—and, if possible, for three months. This is to give us an accurate record of where our money goes, so we can draw up a budget.

Oh, you *know* where your money goes? Well, maybe so; but if you do, you are one in a thousand! Mrs. Stapleton tells me it is a common occurrence for men and women to spend hours giving her facts and figures, so she can get them down on paper—then, when they see the result on paper, they exclaim, "Is *that* the way my money goes?" They can hardly believe it. Are *you* like that? Could be.

Rule No. 2: Get a tailor-made budget that really fits your needs!

Mrs. Stapleton tells me that two families may live side by side in identical houses, in the very same suburb, have the same number of children in the family, and receive the same income—yet their budgeting needs will be radically different. Why? Because people are different. She says a budget has to be a personal, custom-made job.

The idea of a budget is not to wring all the joy out of life. The idea is to give us a sense of material security—which in many cases means emotional security and freedom from worry. "People who live on budgets," Mrs. Stapleton told me, "are happier people."

Rule No. 3: Learn how to spend wisely.

By this I mean: learn how to get the best value for your money. All large corporations have professional buyers and purchasing agents who do nothing but get the very best buys for their firms. As steward and manager of your personal estate, why shouldn't you do likewise? Here are some tips:

1. Write to the Superintendent of Documents, Washington, D. C. Send for a list of government bulletins filled with advice for buyers and consumers. Most of these can be had for a fee of ten cents.

Rule No. 4: Don't increase your headaches with your income.

Mrs. Stapleton told me that the budgets she dreads most to be called into consultation on are family incomes of five thousand a year. I asked her why. "Because," she said, "five thousand a year seems to be a goal to most American families. They may go along sensibly and sanely for years—then, when their income rises to five thousand a year, they think they have 'arrived.' They start branching out. Buy a house in the suburbs 'that doesn't cost any more than renting an apartment.' Buy a car, a lot of new furniture, and a lot of new clothes—and the first thing you know, they are running into the red. They are actually less happy than they were before—because they have bitten off too much with their increase in income."

That is only natural. We all want to get more out of life. But in the long run, which is going to bring us more happiness—forcing ourselves to live within a tight budget, or having dunning letters in the mail and creditors pounding on the front door?

Rule No. 5: Try to build credit, in the event you must borrow.

If you are faced with an emergency and find you must borrow, life-insurance policies and U. S. Treasury Bonds are literally money in your pocket. However, be sure your insurance policies have a savings aspect, if you want to borrow on them, for this means a cash value. Certain types of insurance, called "term insurance," are merely for your protection over a given period of time and do not build up reserves. These policies are obviously of no use to you for borrowing purposes. Therefore, the rule is: Ask questions! Before you sign for a policy, find out if it has a cash value in case you have to raise money.

Now, suppose you haven't insurance you can borrow on, and you haven't any bonds, but you do own a house, or a car, or some other kind of collateral. Where do you go to borrow? By all means, to a bank! Banks all over this land are subject to strict regulation; they have a reputation to maintain in the community; the rate of interest they can charge is fixed firmly by law; and they will deal with you fairly. Frequently, if you are in a financial jam, the bank will go so far as to discuss your problems with you, make a plan, and help you work your way out of your worry and indebtedness. I repeat, I repeat, if you have collateral, go to a bank!

However, suppose you are one of the thousands who don't have collateral, don't own any property, and have nothing to offer as guarantee except your wages or salary? Then, as you value your life, heed this word of warning! Do not—do not—apply to the first "loan company" whose alluring advertisements you see in the paper. These people, to read some of their ads, are as generous as Santa Claus. Don't you believe it! However, there are some companies with nation-wide reputations that are ethical, honest, and strictly on the level. They are doing a service to those people who are faced with illness or emergency and have to raise money. They charge a higher rate of interest than the banks, but they have to do this, for they take greater risks and have greater expenses in collecting. But, before doing business with any loan company, go to your bank, talk to one of its officers, and ask him to recommend a loan company that he *knows* to be fair. Otherwise—otherwise—well, I don't want to give you nightmares.

Rule No. 6: Protect yourself against illness, fire, and emergency expenses.

Insurance is available, for relatively small sums, on all kinds of accidents, misfortunes, and conceivable emergencies. I am not suggesting that you cover yourself for everything from slipping in the bathtub to catching German measles—but I *do* suggest that you protect yourself against the major misfortunes that you know *could* cost you money and therefore *do* cost you worry. It's cheap at the price.

For example, I know a woman who had to spend ten days in a hospital last year and, when she came out, was presented a bill—*for exactly eight dollars!* The answer? She had hospital insurance.

Rule No. 7: Teach your children a responsible attitude toward money.

I shall never forget an idea I once read in *Your Life* magazine. The author, Stella Weston Tuttle, described how she was teaching her little girl a sense of responsibility about money. She got an extra checkbook from the bank and gave it to her nine-year-old daughter. When the daughter was given her weekly allowance, she "deposited" the money with her mother, who served as a bank for the child's funds. Then, throughout the week, whenever she wanted a nickel or a dime, she "drew a check" for that amount and kept track of her balance. The little girl not only found that fun, but began to learn real responsibility in handling her money.

An excellent method! If you have a son or daughter of high-school age, and you want this child to learn how to handle money, here's the title of a booklet I can highly recommend. In fact, it's a *must*. It's called *Managing Your Money* (Consumer Education Series), and it is published by the National Education Association, 1201 Sixteenth Street, Washington, D. C. It has 133 pages of down-to-earth talk for teen-age students—dealing with everything from haircuts to cokes. And it also deals with preparing a budget to help them through college! Cost, thirty-five cents! In fact, if I had a son in high school, I would urge him to read this book and then help *me* frame a family budget.

Rule No. 8: If you are a housewife, maybe you can make a little extra money off your kitchen stove.

If after you budget your expenses wisely you still find that you don't have enough to make ends meet, you can then do one of two things: you can either scold, fret, worry, and complain, or you can plan to make a little additional money on the side. How? Well, all you have to do to make money is to fill an urgent need that isn't being adequately filled now. That is what Mrs. Nellie Speer, 37–09 83rd Street, Jackson Heights, New York, did. In 1932, she found herself living alone in a three-room apartment. Her husband had died, and both of her children were married. One day, while having some ice cream at a drugstore soda fountain, she noticed that the fountain was also selling bakery pies that looked sad and dreary. She asked the proprietor if he would buy some real homemade pies from her. He ordered two. "Although I was a good cook," Mrs. Speer said, as she told me the story, "I had always had servants when we lived in Georgia, and I had never baked more than a dozen pies in my life. After getting that order for two pies, I asked a neighbor woman how to cook an apple pie. The soda-fountain customers were delighted with my first two home-baked pies, one apple, one lemon. The drugstore ordered five the next day. Then orders gradually came in from other fountains and luncheonettes. Within two years, I was baking five thousand pies a year—I was doing all the work myself in my own tiny kitchen, and I was making a thousand dollars a year clear, without a penny's expense except the ingredients that went into the pies."

The demand for Mrs. Speer's home-baked pastry became so great that she had to move out of her kitchen into a shop and hire two girls to bake for her: pies, cakes, bread, and rolls. During the war, people stood in line for an hour at a time to buy her home-baked foods.

"I have never been happier in my life," Mrs. Speer said. "I work in the shop twelve to fourteen hours a day, but I don't get tired because it isn't work to me. It is an adventure in living. I am doing my part to make people a little happier. I am too busy to be lonesome or worried. My work has filled a gap in my life left vacant by the passing of my mother and husband and my home."

When I asked Mrs. Speer if she felt that other women who were good cooks could make money in their spare time in a similar way, in towns of ten thousand and up, she replied, "Yes—of course they can!"

Mrs. Ora Snyder will tell you the same thing. She lives in a town of thirty thousand—Maywood, Illinois. Yet she started in business with the kitchen stove and ten cents' worth of ingredients. Her husband fell ill. She had to earn money. But how? No experience. No skill. No capital. Just a housewife. She took the white of an egg and sugar and made some candy on the back of the kitchen stove; then she took her pan of candy and stood near the school and sold it to the children for a penny a piece as they went home. "Bring more pennies tomorrow," she said. "I'll be here every day with my homemade candy." During the first week, she not only made a profit of $4.15, but had also put a new zest into living. She was making both herself and the children happy. No time now for worry.

This quiet little housewife from Maywood, Illinois, was so ambitious that she decided to branch out—to have an agent sell her kitchen-made candy in roaring, thundering Chicago. She timidly approached an Italian selling peanuts on the street. He shrugged his shoulders. His customers wanted peanuts, not candy. She gave him a sample. He liked it, began selling her candy, and made $2.15 profit for Mrs. Snyder on the first day. Four years later, she opened her first store in Chicago. It was only eight feet wide. She made her candy at night and sold it in the daytime. This erstwhile timid housewife, who started her candy factory on her kitchen stove, now has seventeen stores —fifteen of them in the busy Loop district of Chicago.

Here is the point I am trying to make. Nellie Speer, in Jackson Heights, New York, and Mrs. Ora Snyder, in Maywood, Illinois, instead of worrying about finances, did something positive. They started in an extremely small way to make money off the kitchen stove—no overhead, no rent, no advertising, no salaries. Under these conditions, it is almost impossible for a woman to be defeated by financial worries.

Look around you. You will find many needs that are not filled. For example, if you train yourself to be a good cook, you can probably make money by starting cooking classes for young girls right in your own kitchen. You can get your students by ringing doorbells.

Books have been written about how to make money in your spare time; inquire at your public library. There are many opportunities for both men and women. But one word of warning: unless you have a natural gift for selling, don't attempt door-to-door selling. Most people hate it and fail at it.

Rule No. 9: If we can't possibly improve our financial situation, let's be good to ourselves and stop resenting what can't be changed.

If we can't possibly improve our financial situation, maybe we can improve our mental attitude toward it. Let's remember that other people have their financial worries, too. We may be worried because we can't keep up with the Joneses; but the Joneses are probably worried because they can't keep up with the Ritzes; and the Ritzes are worried because they can't keep up with the Vanderbilts.

Some of the most famous men in American history have had their financial troubles. Both Lincoln and Washington had to borrow money to make the trip to be inaugurated as President.

If we can't have all we want, let's not poison our days with worry and resentment. Let's be good to ourselves. Let's be philosophical. And philosophy, according to Epictetus, boils down to this: "The essence of philosophy is that a man should so live that his happiness shall depend as little as possible on external things." Here is what Seneca said about it: "If you have what seems to you to be insufficient, then you will be miserable even if you possess the world."

And let's remember that even if we owned the world with a hog-tight fence around it, we could eat only three meals a day and sleep in one bed at a time —even a ditch digger can do that; and he will probably eat with more gusto and sleep more peacefully than Rockefeller.

To lessen financial worries, let's try to follow these nine rules:
1. Get the facts down on paper!
2. Get a tailor-made budget that really fits your needs!
3. Learn how to spend wisely.
4. Don't increase your headaches with your income.
5. Try to build credit, in the event you must borrow.

6. Protect yourself against illness, fire, and emergency expenses.
7. Teach your children a responsible attitude toward money.
8. If you are a housewife, maybe you can make a little extra money off your kitchen stove.
9. If we can't possibly improve our financial situation, let's be good to ourselves and stop resenting what can't be changed.

Now It Is Up to You!

GEORGE BERNARD SHAW once remarked: "If you teach a man anything, he will never learn." Shaw was right. *Learning is an active process. We learn by doing. So, if you desire to master the principles you are studying in this book, do something about them. Apply these rules at every opportunity.* Only knowledge that is used sticks in your mind.

Say to yourself: "My peace of mind, my personal happiness, my physical and mental health, and perhaps even my family security, will depend in the long run on whether or not I can make the truths taught in this book a *living* part of my daily existence."

If you want to cure worry—and you *must*, if you value your happiness and health—then set to work at once on applying the principles you have read in this book. Start to apply them by using this 14-day record on the following pages. Every day, for two weeks, answer the questions prepared for you concerning your worries. Give them serious thought. Write down specifically what your worry is about, whether it is "big," or whether it is so small and picayune you are half-ashamed to admit it. Only by nailing down your worry with words can you hope to begin to cure it. Then go on to get the facts about it, to analyze it, solve it. See how this method works—not by taking *my* word for it—but by doing it yourself!

On each page you will find a section marked "2 Weeks Later." That is your proof. Two weeks after writing down your worry for the day, go back and fill in the questions about what really happened. See for yourself how you have steadily developed an ability to *deal* with your problems, and reach a solution.

Let me repeat: *we learn only by doing.* Study this book; read it, and re-read it. Mark in the margins the thoughts that especially apply to your problems. But above all, keep this record. A few minutes a day, for only two weeks—that is a small enough investment, but for results that, I can promise you, *may change your whole life!*

More happiness to you,

Dale Carnegie

14 Day Worry Cure Record

KEEP THIS day-by-day record for two weeks, and watch what it does to your worries.

1ST DAY (WRITE DATE:..)

1. What am I worried about today?

2. Is this worry real or "imaginary"?

3. If real, what can I do about it? (Get all the facts, analyze the facts, list all possible solutions.)

4. Which of these solutions shall I use? (Reach a decision about what you are going to do.)

5. When shall I put my decision into action?

2 WEEKS LATER

(Two weeks later, answer these questions:)

What happened to this worry?
a. What I was worrying about never happened after all, so my anxiety was wasted—(Write details and comments.)

b. The situation solved itself, so I worried about it needlessly—

c. The worry was real, but I solved it myself by doing the following—(Write down fully just what technique you used to solve this worry, and then study this example for future use.)

d. The worry is still unsolved—(If this is so, study the principles in this book again, and, with your added experience, see if you cannot arrive at a solution. If you cannot, read again the chapter, "Co-operate with the Inevitable.")

14 Day Worry Cure Record

KEEP THIS day-by-day record for two weeks, and watch what it does to your worries.

2ND DAY (WRITE DATE:..)

1. What am I worried about today?

2. Is this worry real or "imaginary"?

3. If real, what can I do about it? (Get all the facts, analyze the facts, list all possible solutions.)

4. Which of these solutions shall I use? (Reach a decision about what you are going to do.)

5. When shall I put my decision into action?

2 WEEKS LATER
(Two weeks later, answer these questions:)

What happened to this worry?
a. What I was worrying about never happened after all, so my anxiety was wasted—(Write details and comments.)

b. The situation solved itself, so I worried about it needlessly—

c. The worry was real, but I solved it myself by doing the following—(Write down fully just what technique you used to solve this worry, and then study this example for future use.)

d. The worry is still unsolved—(If this is so, study the principles in this book again, and, with your added experience, see if you cannot arrive at a solution. If you cannot, read again the chapter, "Co-operate with the Inevitable.")

14 Day Worry Cure Record

KEEP THIS day-by-day record for two weeks, and watch what it does to your worries.

3RD DAY (WRITE DATE:......................................)

1. What am I worried about today?

2. Is this worry real or "imaginary"?

3. If real, what can I do about it? (Get all the facts, analyze the facts, list all possible solutions.)

4. Which of these solutions shall I use? (Reach a decision about what you are going to do.)

5. When shall I put my decision into action?

2 WEEKS LATER

(Two weeks later, answer these questions:)

What happened to this worry?
a. What I was worrying about never happened after all, so my anxiety was wasted—(Write details and comments.)

b. The situation solved itself, so I worried about it needlessly—

c. The worry was real, but I solved it myself by doing the following—(Write down fully just what technique you used to solve this worry, and then study this example for future use.)

d. The worry is still unsolved—(If this is so, study the principles in this book again, and, with your added experience, see if you cannot arrive at a solution. If you cannot, read again the chapter, "Co-operate with the Inevitable.")

53

14 Day Worry Cure Record

KEEP THIS day-by-day record for two weeks, and watch what it does to your worries.

4TH DAY (WRITE DATE:...)

1. What am I worried about today?

2. Is this worry real or "imaginary"?

3. If real, what can I do about it? (Get all the facts, analyze the facts, list all possible solutions.)

4. Which of these solutions shall I use? (Reach a decision about what you are going to do.)

5. When shall I put my decision into action?

2 WEEKS LATER

(Two weeks later, answer these questions:)

What happened to this worry?
a. What I was worrying about never happened after all, so my anxiety was wasted—(Write details and comments.)

b. The situation solved itself, so I worried about it needlessly—

c. The worry was real, but I solved it myself by doing the following—(Write down fully just what technique you used to solve this worry, and then study this example for future use.)

d. The worry is still unsolved—(If this is so, study the principles in this book again, and, with your added experience, see if you cannot arrive at a solution. If you cannot, read again the chapter, "Co-operate with the Inevitable.")

14 Day Worry Cure Record

KEEP THIS day-by-day record for two weeks, and watch what it does to your worries.

5TH DAY (WRITE DATE:..)

1. What am I worried about today?

2. Is this worry real or "imaginary"?

3. If real, what can I do about it? (Get all the facts, analyze the facts, list all possible solutions.)

4. Which of these solutions shall I use? (Reach a decision about what you are going to do.)

5. When shall I put my decision into action?

2 WEEKS LATER

(Two weeks later, answer these questions:)

What happened to this worry?
a. What I was worrying about never happened after all, so my anxiety was wasted—(Write details and comments.)

b. The situation solved itself, so I worried about it needlessly—

c. The worry was real, but I solved it myself by doing the following—(Write down fully just what technique you used to solve this worry, and then study this example for future use.)

d. The worry is still unsolved—(If this is so, study the principles in this book again, and, with your added experience, see if you cannot arrive at a solution. If you cannot, read again the chapter, "Co-operate with the Inevitable.")

14 Day Worry Cure Record

KEEP THIS day-by-day record for two weeks, and watch what it does to your worries.

6TH DAY (WRITE DATE:...)

1. What am I worried about today?

2. Is this worry real or "imaginary"?

3. If real, what can I do about it? (Get all the facts, analyze the facts, list all possible solutions.)

4. Which of these solutions shall I use? (Reach a decision about what you are going to do.)

5. When shall I put my decision into action?

2 WEEKS LATER

(Two weeks later, answer these questions:)

What happened to this worry?
a. What I was worrying about never happened after all, so my anxiety was wasted—(Write details and comments.)

b. The situation solved itself, so I worried about it needlessly—

c. The worry was real, but I solved it myself by doing the following—(Write down fully just what technique you used to solve this worry, and then study this example for future use.)

d. The worry is still unsolved—(If this is so, study the principles in this book again, and, with your added experience, see if you cannot arrive at a solution. If you cannot, read again the chapter, "Co-operate with the Inevitable.")

14 Day Worry Cure Record

KEEP THIS day-by-day record for two weeks, and watch what it does to your worries.

7TH DAY (WRITE DATE:...)

1. What am I worried about today?

2. Is this worry real or "imaginary"?

3. If real, what can I do about it? (Get all the facts, analyze the facts, list all possible solutions.)

4. Which of these solutions shall I use? (Reach a decision about what you are going to do.)

5. When shall I put my decision into action?

2 WEEKS LATER

(Two weeks later, answer these questions:)

What happened to this worry?
a. What I was worrying about never happened after all, so my anxiety was wasted—(Write details and comments.)

b. The situation solved itself, so I worried about it needlessly—

c. The worry was real, but I solved it myself by doing the following—(Write down fully just what technique you used to solve this worry, and then study this example for future use.)

d. The worry is still unsolved—(If this is so, study the principles in this book again, and, with your added experience, see if you cannot arrive at a solution. If you cannot, read again the chapter, "Co-operate with the Inevitable.")

14 Day Worry Cure Record

KEEP THIS day-by-day record for two weeks, and watch what it does to your worries.

8TH DAY (WRITE DATE:.......................................)

1. What am I worried about today?

2. Is this worry real or "imaginary"?

3. If real, what can I do about it? (Get all the facts, analyze the facts, list all possible solutions.)

4. Which of these solutions shall I use? (Reach a decision about what you are going to do.)

5. When shall I put my decision into action?

2 WEEKS LATER
(Two weeks later, answer these questions:)

What happened to this worry?
a. What I was worrying about never happened after all, so my anxiety was wasted—(Write details and comments.)

b. The situation solved itself, so I worried about it needlessly—

c. The worry was real, but I solved it myself by doing the following—(Write down fully just what technique you used to solve this worry, and then study this example for future use.)

d. The worry is still unsolved—(If this is so, study the principles in this book again, and, with your added experience, see if you cannot arrive at a solution. If you cannot, read again the chapter, "Co-operate with the Inevitable.")

58

14 Day Worry Cure Record

KEEP THIS day-by-day record for two weeks, and watch what it does to your worries.

9TH DAY (WRITE DATE:...)

1. What am I worried about today?

2. Is this worry real or "imaginary"?

3. If real, what can I do about it? (Get all the facts, analyze the facts, list all possible solutions.)

4. Which of these solutions shall I use? (Reach a decision about what you are going to do.)

5. When shall I put my decision into action?

2 WEEKS LATER
(Two weeks later, answer these questions:)

What happened to this worry?
a. What I was worrying about never happened after all, so my anxiety was wasted—(Write details and comments.)

b. The situation solved itself, so I worried about it needlessly—

c. The worry was real, but I solved it myself by doing the following—(Write down fully just what technique you used to solve this worry, and then study this example for future use.)

d. The worry is still unsolved—(If this is so, study the principles in this book again, and, with your added experience, see if you cannot arrive at a solution. If you cannot, read again the chapter, "Co-operate with the Inevitable.")

14 Day Worry Cure Record

KEEP THIS day-by-day record for two weeks, and watch what it does to your worries.

10TH DAY (WRITE DATE:..)

1. What am I worried about today?

2. Is this worry real or "imaginary"?

3. If real, what can I do about it? (Get all the facts, analyze the facts, list all possible solutions.)

4. Which of these solutions shall I use? (Reach a decision about what you are going to do.)

5. When shall I put my decision into action?

2 WEEKS LATER

(Two weeks later, answer these questions:)

What happened to this worry?
a. What I was worrying about never happened after all, so my anxiety was wasted—(Write details and comments.)

b. The situation solved itself, so I worried about it needlessly—

c. The worry was real, but I solved it myself by doing the following—(Write down fully just what technique you used to solve this worry, and then study this example for future use.)

d. The worry is still unsolved—(If this is so, study the principles in this book again, and, with your added experience, see if you cannot arrive at a solution. If you cannot, read again the chapter, "Co-operate with the Inevitable.")

14 Day Worry Cure Record

KEEP THIS day-by-day record for two weeks, and watch what it does to your worries..

11TH DAY (WRITE DATE:..)

1. What am I worried about today?

2. Is this worry real or "imaginary"?

3. If real, what can I do about it? (Get all the facts, analyze the facts, list all possible solutions.)

4. Which of these solutions shall I use? (Reach a decision about what you are going to do.)

5. When shall I put my decision into action?

2 WEEKS LATER
(Two weeks later, answer these questions:)

What happened to this worry?
a. What I was worrying about never happened after all, so my anxiety was wasted—(Write details and comments.)

b. The situation solved itself, so I worried about it needlessly—

c. The worry was real, but I solved it myself by doing the following—(Write down fully just what technique you used to solve this worry, and then study this example for future use.)

d. The worry is still unsolved—(If this is so, study the principles in this book again, and, with your added experience, see if you cannot arrive at a solution. If you cannot, read again the chapter, "Co-operate with the Inevitable.")

14 Day Worry Cure Record

KEEP THIS day-by-day record for two weeks, and watch what it does to your worries.

12TH DAY (WRITE DATE:..')

1. What am I worried about today?

2. Is this worry real or "imaginary"?

3. If real, what can I do about it? (Get all the facts, analyze the facts, list all possible solutions.)

4. Which of these solutions shall I use? (Reach a decision about what you are going to do.)

5. When shall I put my decision into action?

2 WEEKS LATER

(Two weeks later, answer these questions:)

What happened to this worry?
a. What I was worrying about never happened after all, so my anxiety was wasted—(Write details and comments.)

b. The situation solved itself, so I worried about it needlessly—

c. The worry was real, but I solved it myself by doing the following—(Write down fully just what technique you used to solve this worry, and then study this example for future use.)

d. The worry is still unsolved—(If this is so, study the principles in this book again, and, with your added experience, see if you cannot arrive at a solution. If you cannot, read again the chapter, "Co-operate with the Inevitable.")

14 Day Worry Cure Record

KEEP THIS day-by-day record for two weeks, and watch what it does to your worries.

13TH DAY (WRITE DATE: ....)

1. What am I worried about today?

2. Is this worry real or "imaginary"?

3. If real, what can I do about it? (Get all the facts, analyze the facts, list all possible solutions.)

4. Which of these solutions shall I use? (Reach a decision about what you are going to do.)

5. When shall I put my decision into action?

2 WEEKS LATER
(Two weeks later, answer these questions:)

What happened to this worry?
a. What I was worrying about never happened after all, so my anxiety was wasted—(Write details and comments.)

b. The situation solved itself, so I worried about it needlessly—

c. The worry was real, but I solved it myself by doing the following—(Write down fully just what technique you used to solve this worry, and then study this example for future use.)

d. The worry is still unsolved—(If this is so, study the principles in this book again, and, with your added experience, see if you cannot arrive at a solution. If you cannot, read again the chapter, "Co-operate with the Inevitable.")

14 Day Worry Cure Record

KEEP THIS day-by-day record for two weeks, and watch what it does to your worries.

14TH DAY (WRITE DATE:...)

1. What am I worried about today?

2. Is this worry real or "imaginary"?

3. If real, what can I do about it? (Get all the facts, analyze the facts, list all possible solutions.)

4. Which of these solutions shall I use? (Reach a decision about what you are going to do.)

5. When shall I put my decision into action?

2 WEEKS LATER
(Two weeks later, answer these questions:)

What happened to this worry?
a. What I was worrying about never happened after all, so my anxiety was wasted—(Write details and comments.)

b. The situation solved itself, so I worried about it needlessly—

c. The worry was real, but I solved it myself by doing the following—(Write down fully just what technique you used to solve this worry, and then study this example for future use.)

d. The worry is still unsolved—(If this is so, study the principles in this book again, and, with your added experience, see if you cannot arrive at a solution. If you cannot, read again the chapter, "Co-operate with the Inevitable.")

Recommended Reading

How I made $2,000,000 in the Stock Market
By: Nicolas Darvas

Wall Street: The Other Las Vegas
By: Nicolas Darvas

You Can Still Make it in the Market
By: Nicolas Darvas

How I Made Money Using the Nicolas Darvas System,
Which Made Him $2,000,000 in the Stock Market
By Steve Burns

The Battle for Investment Survival
by Gerald M. Loeb

The Psychology Of The Stock Market
by G. C. Selden

The Science of Getting Rich
by Wallace D. Wattles

Think and Grow Rich
by Napoleon Hill

TRADING SMART: 92 Tools, Methods, Helpful Hints and High Probability
Trading Strategies to Help You Succeed at Forex,
Futures, Commodities and Stock Market Trading
By Jim Wyckoff

Rules Used by Profitable Traders for Investing in Gold and Silver
By Arik Zahb

Available at www.bnpublishing.net

CPSIA information can be obtained
at www.ICGtesting.com
Printed in the USA
BVOW04s2131260617
487496BV00014B/41/P